HUMANS AND DEMONS

HATJE
CANTZ

DISSECTING EVIL IN EVIL TIMES

steirischerherbst'23

Edited by
Ekaterina Degot
and
David Riff

Contents

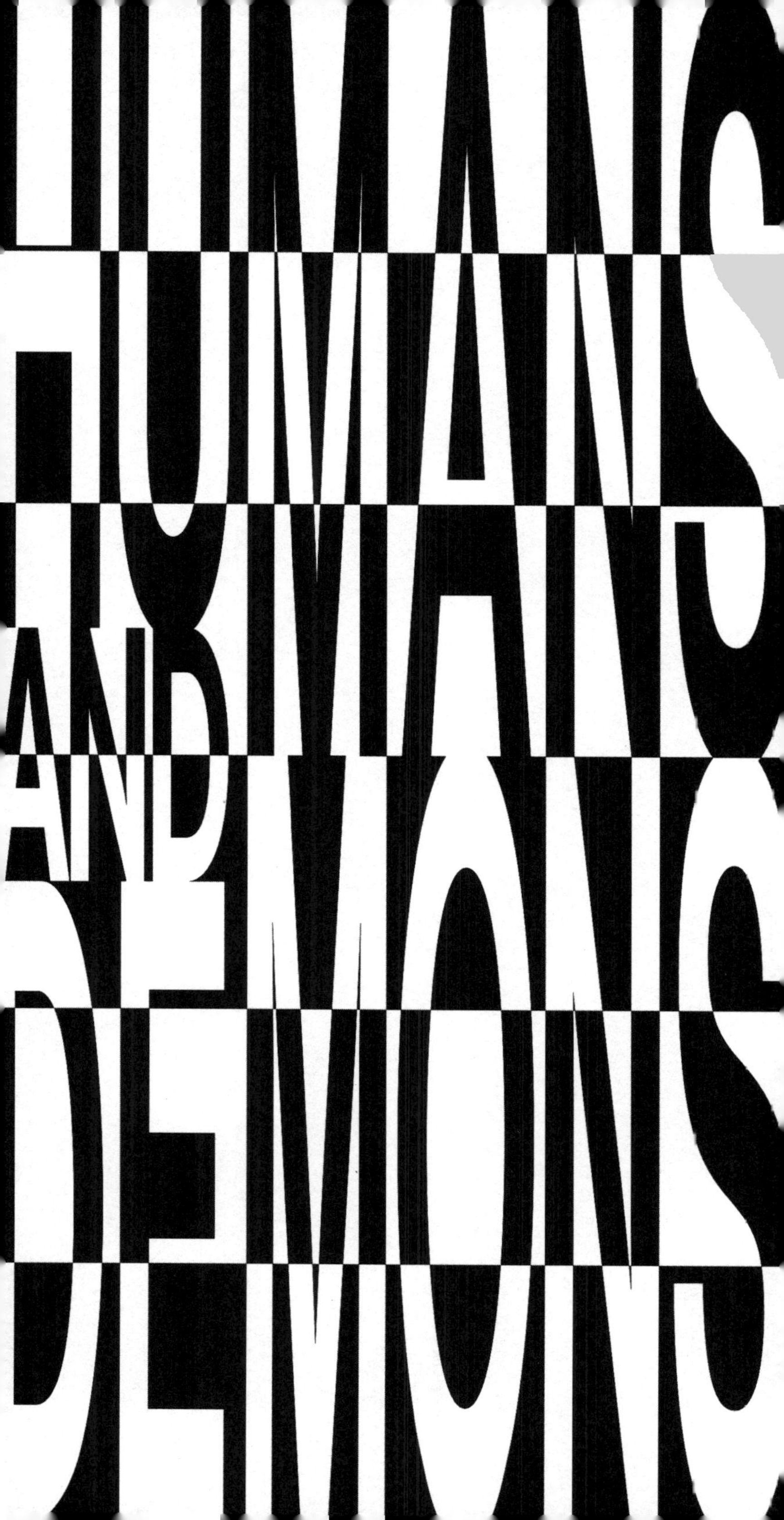

DEMONS
HUMANS
HUMANS
AND
AND
DEMONS
DEMONS

Introduction: Dissecting Evil in Evil Times
Ekaterina Degot and David Riff

For nearly a decade now, *polycrisis* has been one of those notions few writers can avoid. With the COVID-19 pandemic, its frequency seemed to peak, only to unwind into a devastating crescendo of ever greater tragedies since, such as the Russian Federation's full-scale war on Ukraine, which we were still very much preoccupied with as we conceived this project. But something has changed. Recently, the intellectual habit of calling anything that goes wrong a crisis has been replaced by its more pessimistic and perhaps more essentialist version: the discourse of evil.

There is something terribly final in this short word, as irreparable as the crimes and human tragedies unfolding today in Ukraine and Israel and Palestine, as they did in many other regions in the world that got less media attention. With the media omnipresent in our lives, we see evil personified in various truly awful political figures, of which there has been no shortage of late. Evil is everywhere, and by gesturing at it in our knee-jerk statements online, we perhaps only increase its power and prominence rather than fighting it.

Clearly, evil exists, but there are huge problems with how it is conceived. Once evil is personified, the notion shifts, pointing the finger at some concrete monsters and their clique. These monsters are either demons themselves or possessed by demons inevitably called to life by their origin or background. (Is Vladimir Putin so monstrous simply because he is Russian, Soviet, or a former lieutenant colonel of the KGB?) There is a danger in understanding evil as something unique; it precludes any solidarity between those who struggle against it.

The other option, of course, is to admit that evil is not something especially monstrous or unique, but something that lives among us. The most heated debates, extreme conditions, and inhuman crimes polarize all of reality, creating a

15

black-and-white contrast almost physically painful to endure. However, they also produce vast "gray zones" of loopholes, interstices, and oscillating positions. Today, the constant ethical quandaries and complexities of such gray zones are weaponized by authoritarian regimes, especially when the question of collective guilt is involved. The idea that "it's all very complicated" is supposed to make us suspend our judgment. It is paramount to resist that pressure and make ethical judgments nonetheless, to face distributed, diffused forms of evil rather than turning away from them.

The 2023 edition of steirischer herbst, *Humans and Demons*, was conceived against this troubled backdrop, its performances and exhibitions responding to it through complex storytelling involving four complementary characters and various events, all inscribed in a *parcours* across multiple venues in Graz. The artworks and texts related to them appear in a catalogue published separately.

This reader provides insights into the discussions held during the festival and the research process behind it. One focus is on the return of "radical evil," another on the role played by the Putin regime, Russia's wars, and their impact upon the lives of intellectuals and artists displaced by them.

Already in 2013, philosopher Simona Forti wrote an important book called *New Demons*, in which she offers a critical assessment of different but complementary paradigms for understanding evil. One of these Forti calls "the Dostoevsky paradigm": it is based on Immanuel Kant's idea of radical evil and explains evil as an individual desire for godlike omnipotence, often nihilistic to the core. This view of evil only makes sense if one considers the far more banal "mediocre demons" living among us—those willing to allow "necessary" evils to triumph for the sake of preserving and maximizing the petty gains of life. It is the combination of these two that allows evil to prevail, creating gray zones of extreme moral ambiguity. The only way to break through them is to be honest and engage in everyday bravery of the kind found among dissidents of late Socialist times. In conversation, Forti revisits these ideas from a current standpoint.

In his contribution, Graz-based philosopher Peter Strasser expands upon an essay he published in the regional newspaper *Kleine Zeitung* during the festival, responding to its title. Strasser acknowledges that the problem Kant framed as radical evil has returned with a vengeance—and with it the legacies of thinking of evil as an innate quality, to be tracked down, somehow attractive to some for its own sake. Humanity has not forgotten the dark legacies of Cesare Lombroso and his followers. Rather, retreating neoliberal states have outsourced the detection of psychopathologies to arbitrary courts of public opinion. What the public lacks is an ethical instrumentarium, as mutual demonization leads to further violence.

The so-called neoliberal world order creates perfect conditions for outsourcing not only ethics but also thought. In her contribution, historian of technology and digital cultures researcher Orit Halpern explores what she calls "the financialization of cognition" and its effects upon modern financial trading and social media. Today's belief in the self-regulation of algorithms can be traced to a longer neoliberal tradition that sees human intelligence incapable of individual decision-making but self-organizing in neural networks and requiring a certain type of computational machine. "Against the backdrop of civil rights and calls for racial, sexual, and queer forms of justice and equity, the negation of any state intervention or planning (say, affirmative action) becomes

naturalized in the figure of the neural net—a
model of mind and market that appears to make
human-built institutions and organizations
(such as the New York Stock Exchange) seem
like evolutionary, biological necessities. Any
efforts to address structural injustice becomes
a conspiracy against emergence, economy, and
intelligence," Halpern writes.

The same neoliberal order that sanctifies and
naturalizes the market has produced any number
of demonic discourses to vilify those who fail to fit
in. Such developments are especially striking on the
fundamentalist Christian Right in the US (and to
a lesser degree in Europe), who resort to medieval
demonologies to stigmatize entire swathes of
the population. Religious scholar S. Jonathon
O'Donnell has studied this demonology and its
deeper social roots. In their essay, they look at
images of the devil and his servants as shapeshifters
adjusting their appearance to infiltrate and
seduce a society. O'Donnell examines this figure
of "passing" as well as the hunt for and potential
discovery of concealed or assimilated otherness in
a world edging toward a new form of fascism.

Putin and his regime are key to this new
fascism, as one can clearly see in the complex
hybrid war that they currently wage. Their strategy
could be conceived of as a kind of demonic
possession, as artists Anna Engelhardt and Mark
Cinkevich convincingly argue in their contribution. Expanding upon their film *Onset* (2023),
shown at the 2023 festival, they examine how the
Russian Federation's policy of ideological infiltration and military occupation hollows out concepts
and entire countries from within. As artists
from the region living in exile, Engelhardt and
Cinkevich provide a chilling view of an uncertain
future at the hands of Russia's military machine.

Historian and political activist Ilya Budraitskis
is a unique voice among the many intellectuals

18

forced to flee the country following the full-fledged invasion. His essay delves deeper into the role the Putin regime plays in creating the current fascist moment. He shows how this involves a recombination of rapacious neoliberal market forces with ahistorical reenactments of 20th-century history. Historical revisionism and the triumph of postmodern relativism and whataboutism have canceled the results of World War II, creating the conditions for a multipolar world of universal competition over resources and minds. Putin's regime itself constantly displays a "paradoxical combination of voluntarism and fatalism that reveals the profound link between contemporary fascism and neoliberal expediency." It is this link, Budraitskis argues, that makes Putinism so pervasive and infectious: "This regime does not offer the world an alternative project or open the horizon to a shared, albeit frightening, future. On the contrary, it is entirely rooted in the present as an 'endless horror show,' acting as the concentration of the world's fascist moment."

The reader concludes with a selection of literary texts that could be considered reactions to this "endless horror show" of major and minor demons encountered every day.

Poet and performance artist Roman Osminkin fled from Russia with his partner and their infant child, eventually settling in Eastern Germany. His contribution imagines five "plays" for his son: performative-literary renderings of the uncanny situation of living in a context haunted by major and minor demons of the past and present, but also small performances against the victimhood of displacement—something Osminkin clearly rejects.

Franziska Füchsl belongs to a promising young generation of Austrian writers. Her surreal prose piece on single motherhood ironically offers an intricate deconstruction of self-victimization and financialized thinking.

The final contribution is a selection of fragments from the script of Ukrainian artist Dana Kavelina's film *The Lemberg Machine* (2023), a chilling and highly unusual take on the history of the Holocaust in Lviv commissioned by steirischer herbst '23. It ends with a psalm-like passage, a timely prayer against the logic of vengeance and blood feuds prevalent not only in Ukraine today but also in Israel and Palestine—the next site of unimaginable atrocities and scenes of evil since the Hamas attacks of October 7, 2023, and the whole-sale destruction of Gaza by the Israeli military.

21

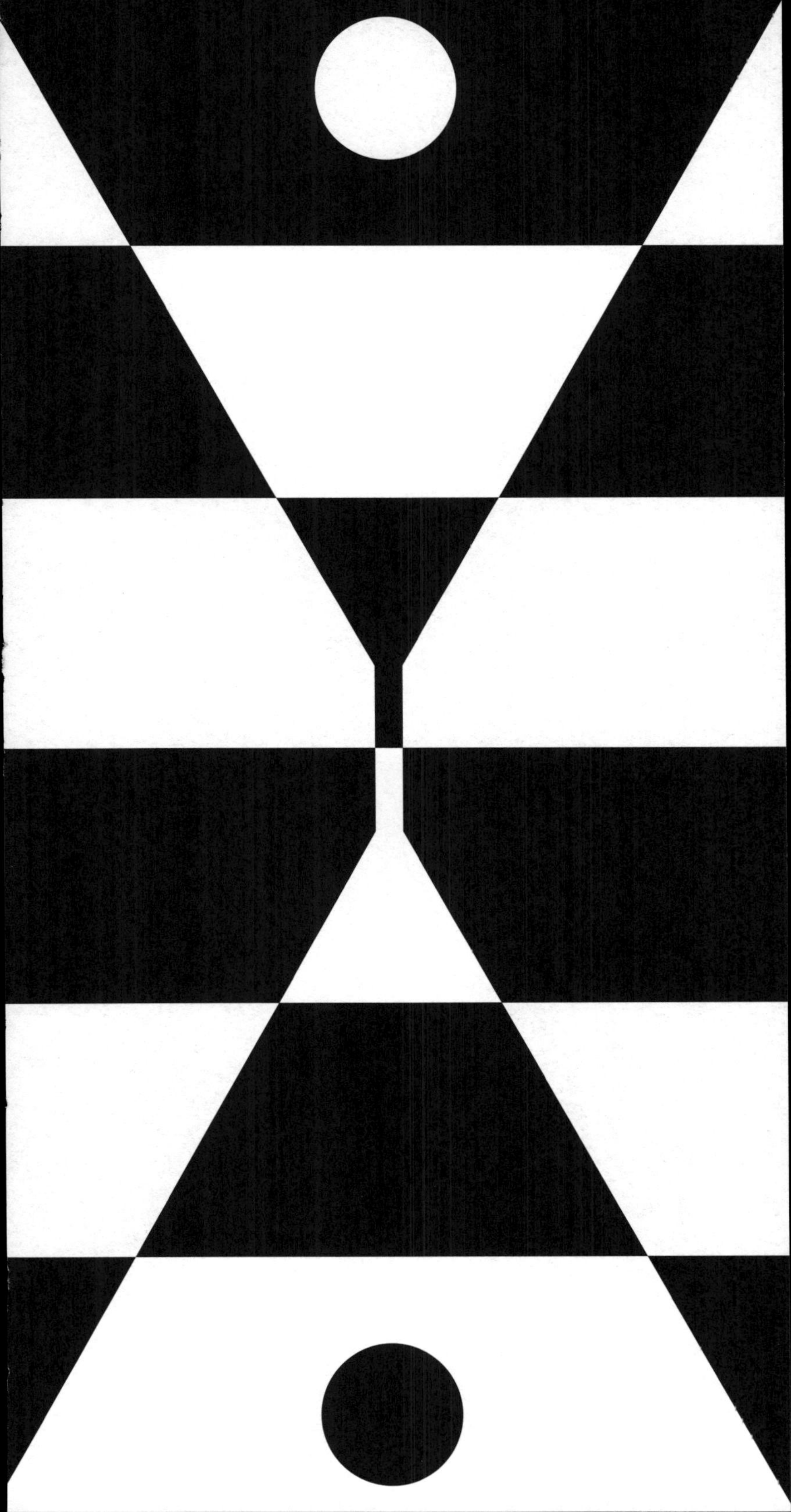

Revisiting the Scene of Evil

Simona Forti in Conversation with David Riff

David Riff (DR): More than a decade ago, you wrote a book about evil called *New Demons*.[1] Could you tell a little bit about what motivated you to write it, and how you saw the situation in the world then?

Simona Forti (SF): The field of political philosophy—with which I am familiar and to which I belong—systematically bans some words and concepts on the ground that their use entails a compromise with metaphysics, dialectics, teleological discourse, and so on. I do not see it that way. These words once had real power in discourse; they have a strength we can recover. In politics and ethics, one of the most potent notions is that of evil. We avoid its use somewhat hypocritically, because we assume that evil exists whenever we pass judgment or ascribe value to our surroundings. I think we need to continue reflecting on evil, even if we are aware that many of the concepts used to think about it are no longer usable.

DR: Enlightened academic discourse avoids talking about evil, while the fundamentalists and neoconservatives do not. Especially over the last decades, they have reweaponized this notion.

SF: Of course, after 9/11, figures like George W. Bush promised to rid the world of evil. The word *evil* was put to polemical and political use to divide the world. If you use the concept this way, it's easy to demand the wholesale destruction of your antagonist. The return of such a dualistic vision was another factor that prompted me to write *New Demons*.

27

DR: The first half of your book is very much
about this dualism. It traces a genealogy
of the notion of evil through what you call
the "Dostoevsky paradigm," which for
you, as I understood, cannot be reduced to
the Russian writer or his cultural context.
What are this paradigm's main features?

SF: If we heed discussions about political
evil, in the classics of political philosophy
and elsewhere, we notice that there is a
similar pattern behind the most diverse
arguments. From the critics of the French
Revolution to today's speeches against
"evil in the world," the question of evil and
the power it unleashes is nearly always
subsumed under the sign of nihilism. Evil
becomes shorthand for unleashing death.
    It was the literary genius of Fyodor
Dostoevsky that gave this nexus between
evil and power its most iconic configura-
tion, embodied in the main characters of
Demons (1871–72). As Dostoevsky writes,
there is a particular logic to evil borne of
the desire to take the place of God and his
infinite freedom. Since finite creatures are
unable to create the world from nothing,
they try to become godlike by reducing
being to nothing, by destroying. This is
how evil enters the world for Dostoevsky
and for the many who, knowingly or not,
follow in his tracks. It signals a condition
where evil is said to emerge as a diabolical
disease of power, a power that, because
it exceeds all limits, can only be the pure
energy of oppression and domination.
This is the basis for thinking about
absolute violence. Of course, Dostoevsky's
conception of evil is much more complex,
but I believe we can talk—beginning

with *Demons*—about the "Dostoevsky paradigm" as a theoretical framework within which many philosophers inscribed the radical evil they saw in the 20th century. It is as if the book offered a transhistorical model, an exemplary scene of evil.

DR: Why is it time to let go of this explanation for radical evil, as you write in the introduction?

SF: If we are talking about political evil, the Dostoevsky paradigm only describes part of the story. It is a unidirectional vision of power that remains faithful to the model of sovereign and subject, whose demonic cypher is the relationship between perpetrator and victim. On one side, there stands an omnipotent subject, bearer of death, and on the other, a subject reduced to a mere object. This translates into the image of an all-powerful leader facing weak, deceived masses.

The phenomenology of power and the scene of evil seem more complex today. Power cannot be represented as a simple, frontal relation. At the same time, political evil is not merely the result of unleashing wickedness. Evil is a network of relations woven between perpetrators, victims, and acquiescent spectators. It is time to look at the world from the perspective of those who accept and prepare the scene of evil, as difficult or uncomfortable as that might be.

DR: This brings us to the second part of your book, on the "mediocre demons" as opposed to the demons of the Dostoevsky paradigm. Can we talk about the difference between the two?

29

SF: For many supporters of the Dostoevsky
        paradigm, power itself is evil, corrupts,
        and already contains a nihilistic drive to
        negate itself. To Michel Foucault, however,
        power is neither good nor evil; rather, we
        are all embedded into power relations
        from the beginning, and these can turn into
        domination if we accept the blackmail of
        those who want to govern us. Everything
        depends upon how we govern ourselves,
        whether we allow relations of power
        to freeze into domination or not. This
        seems to be a realistic appraisal to me.
            Most people, of course, do not
        dream of omnipotence or exhibit a
        drive toward total destruction and
        complete rebuilding. Rather, they want
        to consolidate positions previously
        acquired, to hold on to what they have
        to lose. This is why it is so tempting to
        agree perfectly with someone who claims
        to arrive to save you, to take control of
        your life and save you from death.

DR: So, these neoliberal imperatives of
        self-realization and life maximization help
        to prepare an audience of acquiescent
        and maybe even eager spectators for the
        "scene of evil," as you call it. But the script
        for this scene, it often seems, is a conscious
        reenactment of Dostoevsky. I am thinking
        of Vladimir Putin . . .

SF: "Mediocre" demons do not replace
        "absolute" demons, of course. This is
        not what I mean by my work. Absolute
        demons still exist today, but if their efforts
        are successful, it is because their constit-
        uencies allow this to happen as they try
        to consolidate their lives. Putin is a good

30

illustration of how the two types of demons
work together. He has always played
the bad guy, everyone knew this, and we
didn't need the Russian Federation to
fully invade Ukraine as proof. We already
knew everything around the start of the
new millennium. Nevertheless, Europe
and the US kept to business as usual.
Meanwhile, Putin continues to make a real
show of transgressing limits and physically
violating borders. He is performing evil as
a spectacle for the victim.

Putin is not the only such figure today.
Donald Trump represents a similarly
shameless return of the unlimited. We
might also think about what is happening
in China, India, Argentina, and so on.

These nihilistic politics transcend
national borders and have long since
reached Europe—in Italy, this is obvious. If
they succeed, it is also because we allowed
them to. We need to ask not so much how
we become wicked subjects but, above
all, how we become obedient subjects. We
need to understand what sort of delusions
inspire our feelings of omnipotence, but
even more, we must explain what desire
motivates our anxiety to conform.

DR: It seems to me that COVID-19 also helped
        to prepare people for a very dangerous
        form of unconditional obedience. If
        you were lucky, total obedience to the
        lockdowns paid off with full "life maximi-
        zation," while others were not so lucky and
        had to put their lives at risk.

SF: It's true that the discrimination machine
        was in operation, but it is important to
        stress that the virus was not a metaphor

or an invention to make people more governable. It was a real medical event and very dangerous to some. On our part, it was a gesture of generosity to accept restrictions on some of our liberties to protect fragile people.

DR:	And this generosity you mention was generously rewarded. It was finally possible to bake sourdough bread all you want, or to practice a musical instrument. Neoliberalism often promised such life maximization, but whoever had the time? People were too busy attending meetings at work, engaging in social overproduction.

SF:	The lockdowns were a relief in that regard: this constant pressure to be present and to represent was gone for a while …

DR:	It seems to me that this pressure to signal a position is now back with a vengeance, especially when we examine the dynamic around new scenes of evil. All these events provoke quite standard Dostoevsky paradigm responses in the grand terms of good and evil. Spectators signal what they believe to be virtue, without really caring about the deeper truth. Meanwhile, the mediocre demons prevail. It is very rare to find original positions dissenting from mainstream narratives. Such forms of contrarian truth-telling—disregarding what people in either camp will think— were common among Eastern European dissidents. You write about such thinkers in *New Demons*. Can you tell us a little more?

SF:	The Eastern and Central European "philos- ophy of dissent" has been another taboo

for leftist intellectuals in recent decades;
the dissidents were always associated with
wholehearted support for the transition
to the free market. The real story is more
complex. I wanted to revisit thinkers such
as Jan Patočka or Václav Havel. They show
how individual resistance could become
viral and overthrow a regime, starting
from everyday life. Their thinking can be
very useful in showing how we might break
through a seemingly all-powerful system.

DR: Which is the overall agenda in the second
half of your book.

SF: Yes. Here, I draw upon Foucault's writings
on governmentality and pastoral power,
and even more on the lectures of his later
years devoted to the "care of the self" and
parrhesia, to find some partial answers
to the questions raised by the paradigm
of mediocre demons. First: How is a
relationship of subordination cemented?
What kind of subjectification was
introduced in the Christian West to make
the relationship of care and protection a
perfect mechanism for the production of a
generalized dependency? And also: Under
which conditions is resistance to political
evil possible? Why was an entire field of
experience, from the care of the self to
parrhesia, removed from the spectrum of
examples on which to model our ethical
and political conduct? In a word, does
another way of becoming a subject exist?
    I found the philosophy of dissent
particularly interesting as a kind of
testing ground in this regard. If there is
one thing that really united Charter 77,
for example, it was the conviction that in

33

order for political action to be effective, it can derive only from an ethics. That is to say, political action must be the side effect of an ethos—a position and a conduct—rooted firmly in the habits of the individual's Lebenswelt. The Czechoslovakian dissidents formulated their political critique in philosophical terms. According to them, the gulag, and oppression in general, were not the effect of some demonic essence of Communist power, but rather the result of gestures and daily actions that reinforce each other and ensure the functioning of the regime. It is this area of daily life—and not that of spectacular politics—they sought to intervene in. Foucault and others appreciated this as a rare historical example in which philosophy and an ethos could be actualized into resistance against an omnipresent power.

DR: How should we understand the role of parrhesia—telling the truth—in this ethics-based dissent? To me, "speaking truth to power" always sounds like something grand, heroic, and terrifying—a bit like the Dostoevsky paradigm: an expressive, vivid, and somehow empty drama, detached from everyday life. I guess that is not what you mean.

SF: Parrhesia, in the ancient Greek definition used by Foucault, is a specific mode of speech that chooses "frankness over persuasion, truth over falsehood or silence, the risk of death instead of life and security."[2] The truth spoken here does not have to consider itself absolute or objective, but it is one derived from

34

direct involvement in life, from honesty, and from risk. You say what is true about what you have witnessed, thereby risking to lose something—in the worst case, your life. The point of parrhesia lies in accepting this risk of losing your power or your dependency on power. Foucault uses the example of the Cynics, who renounced all symbols of power and led a "dog's life" as a constant provocation to common sense.

DR: So, a "life in truth" enacts itself daily, on a small, unspectacular level, which is actually where the power of oppressive regimes is located.

SF: Yes. In *The Power of the Powerless*, Václav Havel argues against understanding systems like Socialist Czechoslovakia as dictatorial tyrannies.[3] Rather, he talks about "social auto-totality," enforced daily in a tyranny without tyrants, servitude without masters. His example is that of a Prague greengrocer who displays the sign "Workers of the world, unite!" along with his produce, even though he doesn't believe in the slogan. The grocer complies to ensure a more protected life and thus engages in a kind of "shared humiliation." Parrhesia meant the risk of losing these petty benefits—going on holiday and so on—it wasn't the spectacular risk of prison or death, but it still took a small dose of everyday courage.

DR: One of the strongest descriptions of the lethal implications such petty-privilege hierarchies could have in the 20th century comes from Primo Levi's

35

depiction of life in the camps and the subjectivity it produced. Levi plays an important role in your book.

SF: Primo Levi was the strongest ever deconstructionist of the dichotomy between perpetrator and victim. Of course, there were victims and perpetrators, but we have to differentiate. Especially his last work, *The Drowned and the Saved*, can be read as a refutation of *Demons* and the Manichean conception of power that opens up an abysmal distance between the wicked's feverish will for power and death and the masses' passive obedience.[4] Levi's focus, instead, is on the normal, and yet at the same time perverse, functioning of the gray zone, which, unfortunately, does not only connect opposite sides of the fence at Auschwitz. What Levi says is scandalous, and he was only able to say it as a survivor—namely, that the root of power is our own desire to keep living. Between the absolute victim, the so-called Muselmann, and the all-powerful SS, there are many shades of gray and multiple relations of power, multiple subjectivities with different ways of dealing with power in order to survive. When somebody survived the camps, it was always at the expense of somebody who didn't. This is a very strong assumption of Levi, also about himself.

DR: This seems crucial to me. To Levi, the gray zone is not a moral excuse or a reason to engage in relativization. It seems important to say that, because today's regimes are producing complicity through what Marcia Sá Cavalcante Schuback has called "the fascism of ambiguity."[5] Things

36

are too complicated to understand, so
you should keep quiet and refrain from
judgment. Such nonjudgment is definitely
not what Levi meant.

SF: A normativity of nonjudgment is at work
here, a morality that has so often taught
us that to judge is to echo the first sin our
forefathers committed. So, judgment itself
is already linked to the sin of disobedience.
Nonjudgment probably needs to be
examined as an effective transmission belt
of political evil. As for Primo Levi, he says it
is unreasonable to expect people to behave
like saints or Stoics under the extreme
conditions of the camps. However, these
conditions offer no moral alibi. Levi does
not refrain from judging, and he delivers
his verdict. The number of sadists was
small, but the frustrated were numerous.
These people, he explains, were willing to
collaborate for various reasons: mistaken
judgment, ideological seduction, servile
imitation of the victor, shortsighted desire
for any advantage, cowardice, and so on.
Evil feeds on our ambiguity and blind rev-
erence for authority. And even if a regime
establishes itself through terror, it can only
consolidate itself through compliance.

1   Simona Forti, *New Demons: Rethinking Power and Evil Today*, trans. Zakiya Hanafi (Stanford, CA: Stanford University Press, 2014).

2   Michel Foucault, *Fearless Speech*, ed. Joseph Pearson (Los Angeles: Semiotext(e), 2019), 20.

3   Václav Havel, *The Power of the Powerless: Citizens against the State in Central-Eastern Europe*, trans. Paul Wilson (Amonk, NY: M. E. Sharpe, 1985).

4   Primo Levi, *The Drowned and the Saved*, trans. Raymond Rosenthal (New York: Simon & Schuster, 1988).

5   Marcia Sá Cavalcante Schuback, *The Fascism of Ambiguity: A Conceptual Essay*, trans. Rodrigo Maltez Novaes (New York: Bloomsbury, 2022).

How Do People Become Monsters? On the Topicality of "Radical Evil"

Peter Strasser

41

Today, evil for its own sake seems to have become an object of political fascination again. Are people increasingly falling under the spell of collective demons?

It was not without reason that steirischer herbst '23 was called *Humans and Demons*. For steirischer herbst '93, Catholic scholar Adolf Holl (who died in 2020) and I had already organized a colloquium on the topic "Wie werden aus Menschen Monstren? Wie werden aus Monstren Menschen?" (How do people become monsters? How do monsters become people?).

It was Christianity, humanism, and the Enlightenment that, from the biblical notion of man as an image of God (*imago Dei*), formed the conviction that all people have the same human dignity—even those whose cruel deeds relegate them to the realm of the monstrous. One immediately thinks of Adolf Hitler, Joseph Stalin, Pol Pot, Mao Zedong, and all of today's tyrants who enslave their own people and do not shy away from mass murder. Throughout world history, their names are legion. But insofar as they are human beings, they are, ethically speaking, entitled to the same human rights as everyone else. Recognizing this is difficult to bear, but it is the consequence of our universal moral principles originating in the Sermon on the Mount.

It does not follow that tyrannicide cannot be morally justified under any circumstances. But it is not justified on the assumption that people lack intrinsic human dignity because they are acting— as the saying goes—"beyond humanity," like nonhuman monsters or demons. This clarification is important because, in the 19th century, a supposedly fact-based attitude spread in criminology. It aimed to detect criminals who are biologically determined to antisocial behavior.

Even the naturalistic novel, which otherwise condemned the causes of mass misery and their criminal consequences, could not resist the attraction of this determinism. Painting criminals as biologically driven creatures without free will, these narratives pushed people—especially those with a mental or genetic impairment—to the edge of humanity. Thus, Émile Zola's novel *La Bête humaine* (1890) was based on Cesare Lombroso's theory of the *uomo delinquente*, the "born criminal."[1]

Lombroso, a doctor, psychiatrist, and anthropologist from Turin, is considered to have founded scientific criminology in the last third of the 19th century. He strove to push back speculative criminology in favor of an empirical, controlled study of criminal causes. But at the same time, Lombroso created a new myth best characterized as the "naturalism of evil." Undoubtedly, the scientific method is necessary to ensure objective knowledge, yet objectification can also—and especially—be used to create a particular form of distance toward people.

Lombroso's positivist criminology places habitual criminals and deviant people in a very unfavorable light: their natural dispositions cause them to commit serious crimes. Lombroso claimed that alongside *Homo sapiens* there exists a separate species, the so-called *Homo delinquens*. This anthropological variety is supposedly characterized by several physical stigmata and cranial abnormalities.

A more massive dehumanization is hard to imagine. With experimental and statistical methods, Lombroso wanted to prove that the innate constitution of *Homo delinquens* was linked to psychological pathologies, especially mental weakness, lack of physical excitability, psychological hyperexcitability, moral insanity, and epileptic predisposition.

In the 20th century, Hitler's National Socialism would eagerly seize on this to justify its racial doctrine and the atrocities based on it. Nazi physiognomists even further dehumanized Lombroso's

44

born criminal by using metaphors taken from the world of vermin. Furthermore, they dehumanized non-Aryan humans by drawing upon stories of the devil and infernal imagery. In Hitler's *Mein Kampf* (1925–26), the Jews appear as a demonic race that loves evil for its own sake. They are parasites and bloodsuckers, aiming to bleed their victims dry. Since such vampiric beings have nothing human about them, they also don't have human rights that could protect them from being exterminated like pests poisoning the world …

Today, we see neurobiological research beginning to address the various forms of psychopathy. What older research already suspected seems to be confirmed: it is neither early childhood disorders nor serious deficits in adolescent socialization that lead to antisocial and morally deficient characters, but rather genetic, physiological, and hormonal factors.

For example, imaging techniques reveal that psychopathic criminals exhibit overactivation of certain areas of the forebrain when processing affect-triggering stimuli. In contrast, psychopaths show significantly smaller activity in the limbic system—from which emotional reactions to environmental stimuli originate—than nonpsychopaths.[2]

In 1999, Jan Volavka summed up the neo-Lombrosian view in his article "The Neurobiology of Violence," an update of older research: "The nature-or-nurture controversy that we inherited from Francis Galton was the philosophical basis behind many of the problems that have plagued the field of violence research in previous decades. Recent studies have rendered this controversy irrelevant: Nature is nurture."[3]

This dictum has by no means been generally accepted. Nevertheless, it would be remiss to say that naturalism is outdated as a cause in criminological thinking. For the naturalism of evil fits like a glove in a society that is increasingly

45

moving toward what I would like to call surveillance democracy.

One of the most influential representatives of
the born-criminal tradition is Canadian psychologist Robert D. Hare. He developed the Psychopathy
Checklist (PCL) and the Psychopathy Checklist–
Revised (PCL-R), used to diagnose and predict the
likelihood of violent behavior. In 1995, Hare published *Without Conscience: The Disturbing World
of the Psychopaths among Us*. This popular book
depicts psychopaths in bright colors, namely—in
one of its metaphors—as "social predators."[4] The
danger posed by them is significant.

Some of Hare's alarming, albeit controversial,
numbers and statements are: At least two million
psychopaths are on the loose in North America,
no fewer than one hundred thousand of whom
live in New York City. Twenty percent of the
prison population are psychopaths. More than
50 percent of all serious crimes are committed
by psychopaths. Their recidivism rate is twice as
high as that of other lawbreakers; it is even three
times as high for violent crimes. The number of
psychopaths is constantly increasing because
they are sexually promiscuous and above-average
active; their offspring are also often psychopathic.
Since psychopaths generally don't care about their
children, they can maneuver their genes into a
favorable reproductive position with little to no
personal effort.[5]

What makes matters worse according to Hare
is that our neocapitalist and hedonistic society
is increasingly tolerating traits found on the
Psychopathy Checklist, such as impulsivity, irre-
sponsibility, and lack of remorse. Consequently,
Hare's risk scenario assigns an important role to
so-called subcriminal psychopaths who are socially
successful and never imprisoned.

Among them are a wide variety of
professions: lawyers, doctors, psychiatrists,

academics, mercenaries, police officers, cult leaders, military, businessmen, writers, artists, entertainers. Subcriminal psychopaths are as self-centered, vicious, and manipulative as criminal psychopaths; it's just that their intelligence, background, social skills, and favorable circumstances allow them to put up a facade of normality and get what they want while remaining unpunished.[6]

In 2006, Hare, together with Paul Babiak, a corporate psychologist, published a study on the egomaniac behavior of psychopaths in companies: *Snakes in Suits: When Psychopaths Go to Work.*[7] These types often quickly establish themselves and get to the top, only to leave behind economic disaster after they have ruthlessly exploited their company's resources for some time.

Hare's books show how the naturalism of evil serves a mythology of *them*, that is to say that a group of humans is conceived in such a way that its members ultimately no longer belong to *us*. They encompass all kinds of "monsters": serial killers, terrorists, child molesters, drug pushers, and child and young women traffickers.

The more mythic the struggle between good and evil becomes, the more archaic are the feelings that arise: irrational fears, collectively imagined threats, even doomsday hysteria. Therefore, we need not feel guilty if we deny the "monsters" our human solidarity and compassion. We can demand the harshest punishments for them, even the death penalty.[8]

Fortunately, these are tendencies rather than facts. Nevertheless, the naturalism of evil is not an intra-academic matter but a view that fits our world, just like religious fundamentalism. Hare's vision of psychopaths circulating in everyday life clearly shows eschatological features. The fight against psychopathic danger is reminiscent of Hitler's final battle against "The Jew."

47

I don't mean to claim that we, in the middle of the democratic West, are on the brink of fascism again. To the extent that people participate in and benefit from the market, they know that their personal well-being depends on basic liberal freedoms, privacy, human rights, and social security. The economy "knows" top performances are only possible if people see themselves not as cogs in the machine but as autonomous subjects with a personal responsibility and desire for innovation.

No politician should dare to infringe upon this, at least not overtly. But at the same time, we are witnessing a greater tolerance for security and surveillance technologies, including comprehensive and secret ones. The success of such initiatives depends, among other things, on changing constellations in the legislative bodies, and they point toward a surveillance democracy.

This political tendency is characterized by the state gradually getting rid of its traditional notion of freedom, while still upholding central democratic principles. The classic liberal state, with its staunchly individualist view of humanity, does not simply understand the private sphere as one of nonintervention (where the individual's freedom is expressed in the interplay between rational self-interest and orientation toward the common good). What is more important is the type of nonintervention. Metaphorically speaking, it consists in the state blinding itself.

Its obligation to its citizens demands that the classic liberal state takes appropriate legal and technical precautions so that it is impossible to know what the individual is doing in his or her private life. Yet today, the state's duty to blind itself is increasingly being replaced by the practices of surveillance democracy, on the assumption that surveillance techniques protect the freedom and integrity of law-abiding citizens.

48

These techniques are manifold: they reach from phone tapping, spyware, and location tracking to digital dragnets.

However, when it comes to the need for a certain degree of surveillance in democracies, one should not be naive and ignore the violence around the globe, which does not stop at the West. The eminent Austrian philosopher Karl Popper established that the liberal state must be intolerant of groups that abuse its tolerance to gain power and establish an intolerant rule—a dictatorship.[9] Our societies' development over the last centuries seems to require some surveillance: among the millions of asylum seekers and immigrants in the EU, there are always groups prepared to promote hateful and terrorist actions due to religious or national motives or simply out of a desire for destruction. In addition, the democratic process is increasingly threatened by radical right-wing factions that are beginning to dominate the legislative bodies and undermine the rule of law. However, despite all this, the state should only divest itself of its liberal duties to the extent that maintaining them as is would promote illiberal developments and thus endanger the already shrunken privacy of law-abiding citizens.

The title *Humans and Demons* reflects the current situation in the world. If the 20th century sought to establish the triad of "dignity, human rights, and democracy" in all states of the civilized world, the situation has thoroughly changed in the 21st century. The above-mentioned trinity no longer seems to hold much sway among many ethnic and religious groups. And there are European leaders who—wishing to increase their power—preach the necessity of illiberal measures to save democratic values.

The focus is once again on a form of ethnic collectivism, which necessarily results in a friend/

enemy scheme for peoples or ideologies. They are back, the "others" who are incited by evil desires; they are back, the "demons" that must be destroyed, be it through disempowerment, ghettoization, or physical elimination.

In educated circles in the West, a figure of thought from the Enlightenment philosopher Immanuel Kant is being revived. As is well known, Kant argued that all human dignity arises from the reasoned knowledge about good and evil. Yet, deeply depressed by his time's atrocities, he opened his late work *Religion within the Boundaries of Mere Reason* (1793) with a section about the evil heart of man. From this "heart" flows the urge to do evil for its own sake. Kant spoke of "radical evil," a gratuitous preference for evil.[10]

The temptation to demonize individuals, groups, and entire peoples is incited by climate and pandemic hysteria, disillusionment with democracy, and fear of infiltration by dangerous strangers, coupled with the threat of social decline and obstacles to economic advancement. Today, when radical evil once again seems to penetrate to the very core of our lives, it is—as the populists and nationalists like to say—high time to defend ourselves. Liberal democracy will only survive if effective measures are taken against the demonization of people, regardless of their ethnic origin or religious affiliation.

Unfortunately, ultraconservative Catholic bishops, together with evangelical Protestants in the US, promote a belief in the devil that denounces every liberal thinker as a representative of evil in the world.[11] They no longer reason that all people have the same dignity because—from the Christian perspective—they share the gift of divine grace despite suffering from original sin. Wherever secularization takes root, Christian virtues (love, hope, charity, justice) give rise to a universal ethics of human dignity; the undisputed biblical "So be it!" is transformed into autonomous moral reasoning. The religious hardliners suspect that this is the devil's worst ruse, while they actually fear for their power over people's souls.

But even if one doesn't want to rule out that there could be manifold psychopathic characters in the political arena, there is no reason for today's tyrants and slave drivers to be excused as instinct-driven specimens of *Homo delinquens* (in the Lombrosian sense). Human "demons" are also human beings who, ethically speaking, have the same dignity as everyone else—a dignity that cannot be shaken off to evade moral responsibility.

1   Cesare Lombroso, *Criminal Man*, trans. Mary Gibson and Nicole Hahn Rafter (Durham, NC: Duke University Press, 2006).
2   Kent A. Kiehl et al., "Limbic Abnormalities in Affective Processing by Criminal Psychopaths as Revealed by Functional Magnetic Resonance Imaging," *Biological Psychiatry* 50 (2001): 677–84.
3   Jan Volavka, "The Neurobiology of Violence: An Update," *The Journal of Neuropsychiatry and Clinical Neurosciences* 11 (1999): 307–14, here 313.
4   Robert D. Hare, *Without Conscience: The Disturbing World of the Psychopaths among Us* (New York: Guilford, 1999), xi.
5   Ibid., 2, 87, 96, 70, 166.
6   Ibid., 113.
7   Paul Babiak and Robert D. Hare, *Snakes in Suits: When Psychopaths Go to Work* (New York: HarperCollins, 2006).
8   Hare, *Without Conscience* (see note 4), 143.
9   Karl Popper, *The Open Society and Its Enemies* (London: Routledge, 2011), 581.
10 Immanuel Kant, *Religion within the Boundaries of Mere Reason and Other Writings*, trans. and ed. Allen Wood and George di Giovanni (Cambridge: Cambridge University Press, 2018).
11 Mary Jo McConahay, *Playing God: American Catholic Bishops and the Far Right* (New York: Melville House, 2023).

In the Garden of Speculative Delights: On the Financialization of Cognition

Orit Halpern

55

Starting in the 1960s, and particularly after the 1970s, the New York Stock Exchange (NYSE) and virtually all other financial exchanges became digital, adopting new financial instruments such as derivatives, and later, algorithmic trading. Yet, as late as the 1980s, trading was still a physical act that took place on the floor of the exchange. But by the 1990s, the idea of using architecture to create the "space" of a market appeared contradictory to the dominant trends. The rise of dot-coms, new electronic consumer trading platforms, and new financial instruments had increased the velocity, volume, and automation of trading. Human bodies could no longer register trades fast enough. As a result, the runners and clerks previously managing trades were replaced by traders and "quants" behind Bloomberg terminals and other electronic platforms. These were largely flat screens with graphs and statistical information geared toward actuarial visualization of the market. The need to maintain a "place" for financial exchange was disappearing.

Despite this, in 1997, the Securities Industry Automation Corporation (SIAC), which oversees the technical operations of the NYSE, approached the young architecture firm Asymptote Architecture (Lise Anne Couture and Hani Rashid) to create a "virtual" trading floor, a model or representation of the NYSE that would virtually recreate the exchange space. Asymptote's response to the seeming immateriality of trading was "to turn a physical space into a multidimensional interactive cinematic space." They sought to put "the walls of the Virtual Stock Exchange in motion," as well as, in Cartesian fashion, allow its users to "look at the entire trading floor and fly around it to observe or correlate real-time data."[1] Asymptote's project struggles to integrate the human sensorium into the increasingly immaterial market and offers a new cognitive-perceptual landscape attuned to the imagined future of immersive computing and ubiquitous digital media. Yet, users do not have full information about this landscape, its geography is not clearly demarcated and located.

The market Asymptote modeled was based on a disembodied networked intelligence that culls data from elsewhere and makes decisions autonomously. Traders were not only given a recognizable representation of a space they had known and been in, but also the impression that the market information they received was complete and suitable to ground reasoned decisions. But this Cartesian perspective was only a conduit to be channeled into immersion in the exchange. One struggles to understand where, actually, economic activity is happening. The traders, then, become themselves data for the system, interpolated into the scene only as consumers or perhaps trainees of its intelligence. This model of subjectivity competes with an older assumption of liberal economics that individuals make reasoned decisions based on full information and drove the designers to take inspiration from stories of divinity, namely Hieronymus Bosch's *Garden of Earthly Delights* (1490–1500) and Dante's *Inferno* (1307–21). There is heaven, hell, and purgatory in a market, Asymptote argued, with the exchange itself being "a giant, churning sea of hoarding and wasting."[2]

While the project was not initially framed as modeling an exchange of waste, excess, and information, this has proved prophetic in an age of trading apps, where finance is democratized and YOLOing and HODLing, global macro hedge funds, and options are standard practice. The story of the first virtual 3D trading floor interface shows an emergent and evolving relationship between computing, ideas of networked intelligence, and finance. It offers traces of an attempt to make the market visible to human observers while also developing ways to engage and interact with the market without full information. Asymptote's designs embody an understanding of the market as a flow of networked information, where agency and decision-making is coordinated by machines. The project also exemplifies a broader problem for economists of finance, mainly that theories or models, to paraphrase Milton Friedman, "are engines not cameras."[3] One way to read that statement is that the model does not represent the world, but creates it. Models make markets. A model in finance is something akin to a derivative pricing equation or an algorithm for high-speed trading. There are built-in assumptions about gathering data, comparing prices, betting, selling, and timing bets, but not about whether the information is correct or "true" or whether the market is mapped or shown in its entirety. These models let people create markets by arbitraging price differences without necessarily knowing everything about the market or asset. The instruments are used without necessarily being analyzed or mapped. As a result, models are also not plans. They are understood as ways to act without having to actually direct or build a market through planning by a state or other organization.

Over the past four decades, the idea that both digital machines and human agents are networked intelligences and part of self-organizing systems has not only shaped financial markets, but has also been incorporated into economic thinking and artificial intelligence. This has led to what I call the "financialization of cognition," an economy of attention that reconfigures human agency and decision-making based on a model of contemporary finance and the digital economy. In what follows, I briefly trace some historical precedents of this development and ask about its implications for how we understand our relationships to other people and to the future through finance.

59

Networked Intelligence

Throughout the middle of the 20th century, increased trading volumes had clerks fall behind on transaction tapes and often fail to enter specific prices and transactions. Human error and slowness came to be understood as untenable and "nontransparent," or arbitrary in assigning price. The NYSE also needed ways to manage and monitor labor, particularly lower-paid clerical work. As a result, computerized trading desks were introduced in the 1960s. These were understood as algorithmic and rule-bound. The more automated the market, thinking went, the more rule-bound it would become. Officials also thought computing would save the securities industry from regulation, that if computers followed the rules algorithmically, there was no need for oversight.[4]

This belief in the rationality and self-regulation of algorithms derives from a longer neoliberal tradition that reimagined human intelligence as machinic and networked. According to Austrian-born economist Friedrich Hayek, writing in 1945:

> The peculiar character of the problem of a rational economic order is determined precisely by the fact that the knowledge of the circumstances of which we must make use never exists in concentrated or integrated form, but solely as the dispersed bits of incomplete and frequently contradictory knowledge which all the separate individuals possess. The economic problem of society is thus not merely a problem of how to allocate "given" resources—if "given" is taken to mean given to a single mind which deliberately solves the problem set by these "data." It is rather a problem of how to secure the best use of resources known to any of the members of

society, for ends whose relative importance
only these individuals know. Or, to put it
briefly, it is a problem of the utilization of
knowledge not given to anyone in its totality.[5]

Human beings, Hayek believed, were
subjective, incapable of reason, and fundamentally limited in their attention and cognitive
capacities. The idea that no single subject,
mind, or central authority can fully represent
and understand the world was crucial to how
he conceived the market. He argued that "the
'data' from which the economic calculus starts
are never for the whole society 'given' to a single
mind . . . and can never be so given."[6] Instead,
only markets can learn at scale and suitably
evolve to coordinate dispersed resources
and information in the best way possible.
Responding to what he understood as the
failure of democratic populism resulting in
fascism and communism, Hayek disavowed
centralized planning or states. Instead, he turned
to another model of human agency and markets.
First, Hayek posits that markets are not about
matching supply and demand but about coordi-
nating information.[7] Second, his model of learning
and "using knowledge" is grounded in the idea of
a networked intelligence embodied in the market
that enables the creation of knowledge outside
and beyond the purview of individual humans:
"The whole acts as one market, not because any
of its members survey the whole field, but because
their limited individual fields of vision sufficiently
overlap so that through many intermediaries
the relevant information is communicated to
all."[8] And third, the market therefore embodies a
notion of cognition and decision I would call "environmental intelligence," in which the data pro-
cessed by such a calculating machine is dispersed
throughout society, and where decision-making is

a population-based activity derived from but not congruent with individual bodies and thoughts.

Hayek inherited his idea of environmental intelligence directly from Canadian psychologist Donald O. Hebb, known as the inventor of the neural network model and the theory that "cells [neurons] that fire together wire together." In 1949, Hebb published *The Organization of Behavior*, a text that popularized the idea that the brain stores knowledge in complex networks or "populations" of neurons.[9] Today, his research is famous for presenting a new concept of functional neuroplasticity, developed through working with soldiers and other individuals who had been injured, lost limbs, blinded, or rendered deaf from proximity to blasts. Hebb noted that while these individuals suffered changes to their sensory order, the loss of a limb or a sense would be compensated for through training. He thus began to suspect that neurons might rewire themselves to accommodate trauma and create new capacities.

The rewiring of neurons is not just a matter of attention but also memory. Hebb theorized that brains don't store inscriptions or exact representations of objects but patterns of neurons firing. For example, if a baby sees a cat, a certain group of neurons fire. The more cats the baby sees, the more a certain set of stimuli become related to this animal, and the more the same set of neurons will fire when a "cat" enters the field of perception. This is the basis for contemporary ideas of learning in neural networks. It was also an inspiration to Hayek, who in his 1952 book *The Sensory Order* credited Hebb with providing a key model for imagining human cognition.[10] Hayek used the idea that the brain is composed of networks to remake the liberal subject. The subject is not one of reasoned objectivity, but rather subjective, with limited information and incapable of making objective decisions.

The concept of algorithmic, replicable, and computational decision-making forwarded in the Cold War was not that of conscious, affective, and informed decision-making privileged since the democratic revolutions of the 18th century.[11] But if Cold War technocrats were still experts with authority and predictive capacities, the ignorant and partially informed individual Hayek presents us with is not. He reconceptualized freedom not as the freedom to exercise reasoned decision-making and sovereignty but as the freedom to become part of the market or network. Hayek elaborated that freedom was not willful agency but freedom from coercion. While this could be understood as necessitating legal and humane infrastructures to allow all individuals access to the mythic market, neoliberal thinking and the Republican Party did not interpret it this way.

Machines

If markets and minds are engines, as Milton Friedman implied, then what technical forms might they come to embody?

In 1956, a group of computer scientists, psychologists, and other scientists embarked on a project to develop machine forms of learning. In a proposal for a workshop at Dartmouth College in 1955, John McCarthy labeled this new concept "artificial intelligence." While many of the participants, including Marvin Minsky, Nathaniel Rochester, Warren McCulloch, Ross Ashby, and Claude Shannon, focused on symbolic and linguistic processes, one concentrated on the neuron. A psychologist, Frank Rosenblatt, proposed that learning, whether in nonhuman animals, humans, or computers, could be modeled on artificial cognitive devices that were based on the basic architecture of human neurons.[12]

In his initial Dartmouth paper detailing the idea of a "perceptron," Rosenblatt distanced himself from his peers. These, he claimed, had been "chiefly concerned with the question of how such functions as perception and recall might be achieved by a deterministic system of any sort, rather than how this is actually done by the brain."[13] This approach, he argued, fundamentally ignored the question of scale and the emergent properties of biological systems. Instead, Rosenblatt based his approach on the theory of statistical separability, which he attributed to Hebb and Hayek, and a new conception of networked perception-cognition.[14] According to Rosenblatt, neurons are mere switches or nodes in a network that classifies cognitive input, and intelligence emerges only at the level of the population and through the patterns of interaction between neurons.

Contemporary neural networks operate on these principles. Repeatedly exposed to the same stimuli, groups of nets are trained to eventually wire together. Each exposure increases the statistical likelihood that the net will fire together and "recognize" the object. In supervised "learning," nets can be corrected by comparing their result with the original input. The key feature is that the input does not need to be ontologically defined or represented, meaning that a series of networked machines can come to identify a cat without having to be told what a cat "is." Only through patterns of affiliation does sensory response emerge. The key to learning is therefore exposure to a "large sample of stimuli," which Rosenblatt stressed meant approaching learning "in terms of probability theory rather than symbolic logic."[15] The perceptron model suggests that machine systems, like markets, might be able to perceive what individual subjects cannot.[16] While each individual human is limited to a specific set of external stimuli they are exposed to, a computer perceptron can draw on data resulting from the judgments and experiences of large populations of humans.[17]

64

Adaptation versus Consciousness

For Rosenblatt and Hayek, and their predecessors in psychology, notions of learning forwarded the idea that systems can change and adapt nonconsciously, or automatically. The central feature of these models was that small operations done on parts of a problem might agglomerate into something greater than the sum of its parts and solve problems not through representation but action. Both Hayek and Rosenblatt draw upon theories of communication and information, particularly cybernetics, which conceives communication in terms of thermodynamics and argues that systems at different scales are only probabilistically related to their parts. Calculating individual components cannot represent or predict the act of the entire system.[18] While never truly possible, this disavowal of "representation" continues to fuel the desire for ever larger data sets and unsupervised learning in neural nets that would, at least in theory, be driven by the data.

Hayek himself espoused an imaginary of this data-rich world that could be increasingly calculated without (human) consciousness. He was apparently fond of quoting Alfred North Whitehead's remark that "it is a profoundly erroneous truism ... that we should cultivate the habit of thinking what we are doing. The precise opposite is the case. Civilization advances by extending the number of important operations we can perform without thinking about them."[19] The perceptron is the technological manifestation of the reconfiguration and reorganization of human subjectivity, physiology, psychology, and economy this theory implies. And, as a result of the belief that technical decision-making at the level of populations rather than through governments might remedy the danger of populism or the errors of human judgment, the neural net became the embodiment of an idea (and ideology) that could

65

scale from the mind to planetary electronic trading platforms and global markets.

Historical notions of machine intelligence and networked markets merged in the work of Fischer Black and Myron Scholes and the publication of the Black-Scholes model for options pricing in 1973. This model applied cybernetic communication theories and Brownian motion to market models and exponentially facilitated the automation and computerization of trading in futures and options. In his famous article "Noise," Black posited that we trade and profit from misinformation and information overload. This vision of the market is not one of Cartesian mastery or fully informed decision-makers. Rather, falsity (noise) is the very infrastructure for value. Noisiness creates chances, probabilities, and volatility that can be bet on or arbitraged: "Noise in the sense of a large number of small events is often a causal factor much more powerful than a small number of large events can be. Noise makes trading in financial markets possible, and thus allows us to observe prices for financial assets."[20]

Black's statement refracts and consolidates thirty years of research in computing, psychology, and economics that reconfigured ideas of decision-making away from liberal or enlightenment reason. In 1990, Andrei Shleifer and Lawrence H. Summers drew the conclusion that, from the market's perspective, truth or reality might not only be impossible to represent but irrelevant—a conclusion that drove the use of derivative instruments.[21] It is important to note that this theory of networked noisiness and speculation on volatility came with the end of Bretton Woods, decolonization, post-Fordism, and the OPEC oil crisis, to name but a few of the transformations at the time.

The derivative pricing equation emerged, then, as a way to tame or circumvent extreme volatility in politics, currency, and commodity markets.

66

New financial technologies and institutions such as computer-driven trading and hedge funds were created in order to literally "hedge" bets: to ensure that risks were reallocated, decentralized, and networked. Through the likes of short bets, credit swaps, and futures markets, dangerous bets could be combined with safer ones and dispersed across multiple territories and temporalities. Corporations, governments, and financiers flocked to these techniques of uncertainty management in the face of unnameable, and unquantifiable, risks.[22] In this world, volatility, noise, and chance were no longer "devils," in the words of cybernetician Norbert Wiener, but rather media with value.[23] The impossibility of prediction, the subjective nature of human decision-making, and the electronic networking of global media systems, all became infrastructures for new forms of betting on futures.

Models, Machines, and Infernos
Neoliberal economics often theorizes the world as a self-organizing adaptive system to counter the idea of planned and perfectly controllable political (and potentially totalitarian) orders. Within this ideology, the market takes on an almost divine, or perhaps biologically determinist, capacity for chance and emergence, but never through consciousness or planning.[24] Evolution is imagined against willed action and the reasoned decisions of individuals. More critically, against the backdrop of civil rights and calls for racial, sexual, and queer forms of justice and equity, the negation of any state intervention or planning (say, affirmative action) becomes naturalized in the figure of the neural net—a model of mind and market that appears to make human-built institutions and organizations (such as the NYSE) seem like evolutionary, biological necessities. Any efforts to address structural injustice becomes a conspiracy against emergence, economy, and intelligence.[25]

67

We have become attuned to this model of the
world where our machines and markets are synco-
pated with one another. As an ideology, a model of
mind and markets, and a technology, neural nets
might have cyborg potentials in Donna Haraway's
sense of the term. As cultural theorist Randy
Martin has argued, rather than separating itself
from social processes of production and reproduc-
tion, algorithmic finance actually demonstrates
the increased interrelatedness, globalization,
and socialization of debt and precarity.[26] By tying
together disparate actions and objects into a single
assemblage of reallocated risks for trading, new
market machines have made us more indebted
to each other. The political and ethical question
then becomes: How might we activate this mutual
indebtedness in new ways, ways less amenable to
the strict market logics of neoliberal economics?

The future lies in recognizing what our
machines have finally made visible, and what has
perhaps always been there: the sociopolitical
nature of our seemingly natural thoughts and
perceptions. Every market crash, every subprime
mortgage event reveals the social constructedness
and the work—aesthetic, political, economic—it
takes to maintain our belief in markets as forces
of nature or divinity. And if not aesthetically
smoothed over through media and narratives of
inevitability, they also make it possible to recognize how our machines have linked so many of us
together in precarity. The potential politics of these
moments has not yet been realized, but there have
been efforts, whether in Occupy or more recently
in movements for civil rights, racial equity, and
environmental justice such as Black Lives Matter or
the Chilean anti-austerity protests of 2019.

If we consider that all computer systems are
programmed, and therefore planned, we are
also forced to contend with the intentional and
therefore changeable nature of how we think and

perceive our world. Asymptote's failed efforts to build a visualization of the market, birthed new modes of interactivity, making us recognize the historically situated and socially specific nature of both the economy and attention. "We are now at the threshold of an uncharted landscape," wrote Asymptote, "well beyond the sanctuary of order and reason. Here concealed beyond places inviting yearning and anticipation, we discover an architecture that perseveres."[27] This architecture that might produce relations and futures other than those of capital did not appear on the virtual trading floor, but perhaps it still might in other forms and practices. Architecture must attend to its own aesthetic political economy.

Research for this article was supported by the Mellon Foundation, Digital Now Project, at the Center for Canadian Architecture (CCA), and by the staff and archives at the CCA. Further funding was given by the Swiss National Science Foundation, Sinergia Project, Governing Through Design.

1 Lise Anne Couture, Hani Rashid, and Gregg Lynn, *Asymptote Architecture: NYSE Virtual Trading Floor; Oral History*, ed. Greg Lynn (Montreal: Canadian Center for Architecture, 2015), 40.

2 Ibid., 44.

3 Donald A. MacKenzie, *An Engine, Not a Camera: How Financial Models Shape Markets* (Cambridge, MA: MIT Press, 2006).

4 Devin Kennedy, "The Machine in the Market: Computers and the Infrastructure of Price at the New York Stock Exchange, 1965–1975," *Social Studies of Science* 47, no. 6 (2017): 888–917.

5 F. A. Hayek, "The Use of Knowledge in Society," *The American Economic Review* 35, no. 4 (1945): 519–30, here 519–20.

6 Ibid., 519.

7 A critical first step, as historians such as Philip Mirowski have noted, toward contemporary notions of information economies. Philip Mirowski, *Machine Dreams: Economics Becomes a Cyborg Science* (Cambridge: Cambridge University Press, 2002); Philip Mirowski, "Twelve Theses Concerning the History of Postwar Neoclassical Price Theory," *History of Political Economy* 38 (2006): 344–79.

8 Hayek, "The Use of Knowledge in Society" (see note 5), 526.

9 Donald O. Hebb, *The Organization of Behavior: A Neuropsychological Theory* (New York: Wiley, 1949).

10 F. A. Hayek, *The Sensory Order: An Inquiry into the Foundations of Theoretical Psychology* (Chicago: The University of Chicago Press, 1952).

11 Paul Erickson et al., *How Reason Almost Lost Its Mind: The Strange Career of Cold War Rationality* (Chicago: The University of Chicago Press, 2015).

12 Frank Rosenblatt, *Principles of Neurodynamics: Perceptrons and the Theory of Brain Mechanisms* (Washington, DC: Spartan, 1962).

13 Frank Rosenblatt, "The Perceptron: A Probabilistic Model for Information Storage and Organization in the Brain," *Psychological Review* 65, no. 6 (1958): 386–408, here 388.

14 Ibid.

15 Ibid.

16 Ibid., 388–89.

17 Frank Rosenblatt, *Principles of Neurodynamics* (see note 12), 19–20.

18 For more on the influence of cybernetics and systems theories on producing notions of nonconscious growth and evolution in Hayek's thought, see Paul Lewis, "The Emergence of 'Emergence' in the Work of F. A. Hayek: A Historical Analysis," *History of Political Economy* 48, no. 1 (2016): 111–50; Gabriel Oliva, "The Road to Servomechanisms: The Influence of Cybernetics on Hayek from 'The Sensory Order' to the Social Order," *Research in the History of Economic Thought and Methodology* 34 (2016): 161–98.

19 Alfred Moore, "Hayek, Conspiracy, and Democracy," *Critical Review* 28, no. 1 (2016): 44–62, here 50. I am indebted to Moore's excellent discussion for much of the argument surrounding Hayek, democracy, and information. The quote is from Hayek, "The Use of Knowledge in Society" (see note 5), 528.

20 Fischer Black, "Noise," *The Journal of Finance* 41, no. 3 (1986): 529–43.

21 Andrei Shleifer and Lawrence H. Summers, "The Noise Trader Approach to Finance," *The Journal of Economic Perspectives* 4, no. 2 (1990): 19–33.

22 For an excellent summary of these links and of the insurance and urban planning fields, see Kevin Grove, *Resilience* (New York: Routledge, 2018).

23 For an extensive discussion of thermodynamics, stochastic processes, and control, see the introduction of Norbert Wiener, *Cybernetics, or Control and Communication in the Animal and the Machine* (New York: MIT Press, 1961). For further discussion, see also Orit Halpern, "Dreams for Our Perceptual Present: Temporality, Storage, and Interactivity in Cybernetics," *Configurations* 13, no. 2 (2005): 283–319; Peter Galison, "The Ontology of the Enemy: Norbert Wiener and the Cybernetic Vision," *Critical Inquiry* 21 (1994): 228–66.

24 Joshua Ramey, "Neoliberalism as a Political Theology of Chance: The Politics of Divination," *Palgrave Communications* 1 (2015): http://dx.doi.org/10.1057/palcomms.2015.39.

25 Michael Schaus, "Narrative & Value: Authorship in the Story of Money," ResearchGate, August 2017, https://www.researchgate.net/publication/328411995_Narrative_and_value_authorship_in_the_story_of_money.

26 Randy Martin, "What Difference Do Derivatives Make? From the Technical to the Political Conjuncture," *Culture Unbound* 6 (2014): 189–210.

27 Hani Rashid and Lise Anne Couture, *Asymptote: Architecture at the Interval* (New York: Rizzoli, 1995), 49.

Demon-ologies of Passing in an Age of Reactionary Politics

S. Jonathon O'Donnell

73

In the fourth book of John Milton's 1667 epic poem *Paradise Lost*, the devil comes to Eden. Initially, he stalks about its walls. Eventually tiring of this circumambulation, he bounds over them like a prowling wolf. This is not the only bestial mode he takes, however. He both acts like and adopts the semblance of beasts, shifting through multiple animal forms. First, he is a cormorant. Then an unnamed quadruped grazer, a toad, and finally the infamous serpent. Bird, mammal, amphibian, reptile. In a place where he does not belong, Satan passes as those that do. Yet his state in paradise is fitful and protean, a state that literary scholars have interpreted as reflecting both the devil's deep anxiety about continuity and a wider demonic rejection of the fixity and permanence of heaven itself. However, it is paradise's continuity that is threatened by the trespassing of this passing figure. Satan traverses the borders of paradise, revealing their porosity. He adopts the semblance of its occupants, unfixing its fixity. There is a cascading consequence for his actions: a story of temptation and fall, of the rejection of divine commandment and its consequences, and of eternity surrendering to the flow of time. His dissent occasions the descent.

The passage of the devil here marks the limits of paradise and its possibility. It marks what should not be—a deviation from proper order. Satan comes from outside, unsettling the stasis of divine order and thereby inaugurating its collapse. But Satan is not simply from outside. Rather, he is a former insider—an angel who has rejected his proper place and purpose, and who in that rejection brings ruination to the original, and natural, order of the cosmos. It is perhaps for this reason that the walls of paradise fail to guard against him. He knows their shape and structure, their inability to secure themselves from all angles and avenues of infiltration. However, the fact that paradise has walls at all is important. The English word *paradise*

75

stems from the Greek *parádeisos* (itself from the Avestan *pairidaēza*), which referred to the concept of a walled garden—specifically the walled gardens of the monarch, the royal enclosure. A paradise housed the king's arboretums and menagerie, the assortment of plants and animals that were acquired from within and beyond the borders of the kingdom, curated and cared for by the sovereign and his subjects. As such, the paradise was a microcosm of the sovereign's power and the territory of his dominion. It was a symbol of sovereignty, and through holding (or seeking to hold) beings from across the sovereign lands, carried with it an imperial resonance—a desire for both expansion and enclosure, for the ever-growing acquisition of new life to fill the walled gardens and the need to secure those same walls lest their inhabitants become targets of a recusant—perhaps even diabolic—sneak thief.

I begin with this scene from *Paradise Lost*, and with the concept of paradise more generally, because to me they speak to us of the present moment: of patterns of demonization, securitization, and imperial capture, of the anxieties about the alleged erosion of an ostensibly natural or "normal" state of being by dark forces. That *Paradise Lost* is a retelling of a Christian, and a Western Christian, story is not coincidental here. I am primarily an academic who studies modern Christianity and Christianity's relationship to "the West" as a cultural and historical concept. As such, it is to Europe and America that my attention is primarily drawn, where the cultural and political zeitgeist is often informed by the history and hold of Christianity and its narratives. The figure of the devil is part of this history, as are the narrative tropes and theological concepts associated with him. The devil tempts individuals from the proper path, but often he does not do so openly. Even Satan can "masquerade as an angel of light," 2 Corinthians 11:14 informs us. The 1864 prose poem by Charles Baudelaire, "The Generous Gambler," memorably informs narrator and audience that the greatest trick the devil can pull is convince you he doesn't exist. The devil traditionally comes to us when we are unawares, and it is thus dissimulated that he poses his greatest threat to our lives and livelihoods, our mortal selves and immortal souls.

Inasmuch as deceptive appearances—and the loss of security or salvation these deceptions lead to—are a central feature of the devil's character, fears of counterfeiting and of dissimulation have often been prominent aspects of social patterns of demonization in the West, especially in modernity. The notion that specific social others may be masquerading under the guise of the self provokes anxiety among those populations who hold their power and privilege to be the norm—due to a perceived sense of innate identity. We see this historically in anxieties around the concept of passing, whether this is understood in racial, sexual, religious, or gendered terms. To "pass" is to be perceived as something you "are not," often in a way that grants the passing subject rights or privileges based on that perception. The term *passing* is thought to have arisen historically in relation to racial ordering in the United States, in which it was possible for lighter-skinned African Americans to "pass" through racially policed checkpoints. They were perceived as white, passed as white, and were given privileges of mobility because of that. Since then, the concept has been extended to other categories of identity, including sexuality (where a queer person might pass as heterosexual) and gender (where a trans person might pass as cisgender). In all, an individual from a marginalized identity group is perceived as a member of the dominant group. This perception can be beneficial to the individual, preserving them from harassment and discrimination (however temporarily), but it can also be alienating, forcibly separating them from their community, their history, their identity. To the dominant group, however, the passing figure is often a figure of anxiety—one that reveals that the boundaries of normalcy and the hierarchies of race and gender on which that vision of normalcy relies.

A racialized person "passing" as white or a transgender person "passing" as cisgender unsettles the societal divisions and assumed naturalness on which racial and gendered hierarchies depend. In doing so, such individuals threaten the systems of power (material and discursive) that act to enforce these hierarchies, provoking anxieties in those who benefit from these systems and their maintenance. As a result, passing individuals are marked as threats—people to be identified and then excluded or eliminated. This identification relies on creating and reinforcing processes of policing, securitization, and surveillance—passing subjects must be rooted out. At the same time, they rely on notions of time. Passing is always assumed to be transitory, passing in time as well as through space. The passing subject is seen by society as living on borrowed time, the exposure of what they "really are" being inevitable, and so the rights and privileges they gain by passing are always revocable upon discovery of the "truth" of their nature. In this view, a white-passing Black person or a cis-passing trans person will always reveal themselves somehow, by some mannerism or physiological feature that exposes an eternal, unchanging essence. This is false, however. There is no absolute, necessary reason why someone who passes must ever be exposed, no striking feature that has to reveal them as what they "really are." The belief that there must be is a fiction, one that reassures the dominant group that their privilege and power—as white, as cis, as straight—is based on some natural quality, rather than merely historical contingency and societal perception. The trespass of the passing figure threatens the serenity, stasis, and stability of the paradise they have built for themselves.

I should clarify that I do not in any way here seek to imply that people who pass are evil, demonic, or the devil himself. Passing is an often painful and alienating strategy of survival. However, to the dominant group, people who pass can sometimes take on the image of the demonic, a hidden threat that challenges the group's way of life. This can be as much or even more the case if the passing figure is imagined, something that can easily be seen if one looks at the landscape of current reactionary politics and right-wing culture wars. In my homeland of the United Kingdom, for example, reactionary political forces energized by Brexit have filled the political mainstream with attacks on marginalized groups accused of infiltrating spaces and acquiring benefits they "should" not possess, thereby threatening the alleged integrity of British society. Claims about "bogus" asylum seekers and undocumented migrants gaining illegitimate access to the nation and its resources have long been staples of right-wing scaremongering, portraying the nation as a fortress to be defended from assault. In recent years, anti-immigrant rhetoric has been joined by a rising chorus of transphobia that has captured the right and the center, portraying trans women as deceptive predators seeking to gain illicit access to "women's spaces" and trans men as impressionable young girls tempted astray by peer pressure and the "social contagion" of "gender." Like anti-immigrant rhetoric, this language, and the fears it evokes, are not recent. In addition to replicating deep patterns of traditional patriarchal misogyny, one of predatory "men" and vulnerable "girls," they

79

echo the moral panics around homosexuality
of the 1990s—ones I grew up with. In these, the
imagined figure of the predatory homosexual
lurked behind every corner and threatened
to corrupt impressionable youth, leading to
legislation such as Section 28, which banned open
discussions of homosexuality in public life and
professions. In both moral panics, the proposed
solution is portrayed as a defense of the "natural"
and the "normal," a return to a mythical time
when "men were men" or when we "knew what
a woman was," as a means of restabilizing an
image of society that sees itself as under threat.
This solution seeks to impose a social order that
presents itself as natural, where everything is
fixed and as it seems, in a manner that corresponds to a reactionary image of a paradisial
past. It builds a walled garden within which
everything must be tamed and whose boundaries
must be defended at all costs.

This surge in far-right ideology has sadly not
been contained to the United Kingdom, but has
become ascendant across both Europe and the
United States as well as elsewhere in the world.
Nor are such moral panics around gender and
sexuality, as well as immigration, unrelated.
Often articulated by the same individuals and
organizations, they become linked more directly
as reactionary movements portray an alleged
feminization of "Western" culture as leading to
its infiltration and subversion by the "non-West."
Islamophobia and antisemitism are often a core
pillar of these claims, albeit in distinct ways. One
common claim focuses on the alleged vulnerability
of white women to virile and violent Black or
brown Muslim men, released onto the West by
increasingly lax immigration laws enforced (or
rather not) by effeminized white men who have
been forced (by a decadent culture or political
correctness) to forego their masculinity. It is here

that antisemitism comes into play, as these visions
of cultural and demographic "replacement" are
imagined as the conspiratorial plans of shadowy
cabals of—frequently Jewish—elites aiming
to destroy "the West." The conspiracy theories
around liberal Jewish billionaire George Soros,
whose name has become synonymous with such
notions across the far right in Europe and America
over the past decade, epitomize these claims. This
is not new, of course: modern antisemitism has
long sought to cast Jewish people as dangerous,
parasitic, and conniving others seeking to destroy
the fabric of Western, Christian society, especially
after the Jewish Enlightenment or Haskalah of the
18th and 19th centuries led to wider Jewish inte-
gration in European public and political life. While
Jewish people had long been viewed by Christian
Europeans powers as "internal outsiders"—people
who lived in Christendom but were not of
Christendom, indeed, who were often viewed as
diabolical agents that threatened Christian civilization from the inside—new narratives emerged
in modernity that sought to paint modern Jews
as passing figures. Modern antisemites still saw
Jewish people as diabolic in nature, but leveraging
a growing insider status to destroy European
Christendom from the inside. Muslims, meanwhile,
were positioned as the enemy without—the
barbaric and yet enticing other beyond the edges
of Christian civilization against which the norms of
society could be defined.

While this has continued to be a defining
feature of white Christian demonization of its
religious others, the demographic changes in
Europe over the latter half of the 20th century have
also coincided with Islam's portrayal as an internal
threat. A prominent subset of Islamophobic
ideas emerging from reactionary spaces revolves
around the Islamic concept of *taqiyyah*—a survival
strategy from Shiite Islam that holds that Muslims

may conceal their faith if revealing it would place them or their loved ones in mortal peril. That is, when one's life is under threat, a Muslim may attempt to "pass" as non-Muslim, or—since Shiite Islam was itself historically persecuted by the Sunni majority—as a different kind of Muslim. In the hands of the far right, *taqiyyah* has taken on a life of its own, however. To those who wish to portray Islam as an existential threat to "the West" and its way of life, *taqiyyah* becomes something sinister, even diabolic. It is used to justify the idea that all Muslims lie—indeed, that it is the very nature of their religion to lie—and that Muslims who are politically or religiously moderate, or adopt aspects of Western culture and social norms, are merely biding their time, infiltrating European or American society until they can destroy it from within. This Islamophobic demonization takes a survival strategy linked to one specific version of Islam and depicts it as not simply universal to all Muslims but as the alleged essence of their religion, one that makes them fundamentally incompatible with Western society and their continued existence within it a threat that must be removed. Muslims are rendered merely passing figures: figures who are passing as what they "are not" but also passing into spaces they "should not" be in and, ultimately, passing in time, destined for exposure and removal so that "proper order" can be restored.

As with the above examples regarding immigrants or gender and sexual minorities, these anti-Muslim and antisemitic conspiracy theories ascribe sinister motives to minorities, casting them as existential threats to society. It also reveals the way that reactionary belief systems rely on notions of essence: immigrants, transgender people, Muslims, and Jews are depicted as essentially and intrinsically threatening, their nature incompatible with the norms and values of "proper" society, up to the concept of truth itself. This is the diabolic threat that is projected onto the passing figure, whether real or imagined—those whose very existence is assumed to be inauthentic, whose presence threatens to destabilize everything but especially "the way that things should be": the racial, gender, or religious hierarchy, the imagined cultural essence, and the normal order of politics as usual. Passing individuals are portrayed as counterfeits who move through society as counterfeit money circulates through an economy, undermining it from within. The result is a desperate need for greater security and surveillance, and both fueling it and fueled by it is the fear of access—of existence—being granted to the "wrong" people, the ones whose entry into or acceptance by society would risk compromising some state of existence deemed natural and eternal yet apparently under constant threat and needing to be defended at all costs. Like Satan in *Paradise Lost*, passing figures are cast as devils gaining illicit entry into paradise, their refusal or inability to comply with the demands of a society that has already decided to exclude them becoming threats to that paradise's possibility and perpetuity.

It is important to call these politics what they are: fascist. Like all breeds of fascism, they imagine enemies from within and without, seeking to eliminate both in the violent pursuit of an imaginary sense of purity and singularity. They chase ghosts of an imagined past, but create real flesh-and-blood victims. They imagine demons, and give birth to practices of demonization, of dehumanization, that project those demons onto people they see as others. It is important to stress fascism's capacity to imagine demons, and the history of demons it draws on in this imagination. The devil is in many ways the prototypical fascist other, denied the possibility to create the original or authentic foundations of any social or political order and portrayed as capable only of the destruction of

83

the great, the good, and the beautiful. Similarly, much as fascists imagine their enemies as both weak and strong—as an existential threat to "our" society and future and yet also innately inferior, without intrinsic value, and so unable to build a society or future of their own—the devil, too, has historically and theologically been envisioned as weak and strong. On the one hand, the devil is a threat to one's immortal soul, leading one away from paradise toward eternal damnation. On the other hand, he is already defeated in the Christian narrative of history—both by Christ through his resurrection and victory over death and in the predestined apocalyptic future where he is to be cast into the lake of fire before the world is reborn. A contingent and created being, the devil cannot traditionally create for himself, but is rather forced to subvert divine power for alternative ends. Cast out of Heaven for his crimes and therefore out of the fullness of divine plenitude and power, the evil he embodies is conceived as an absence or void—something that can only exist by parasitizing the good, incapable of existing on its own terms.

Like the devil in traditional Christian theology, the others imagined in fascist politics are framed as lacking in independent creative capacity, capable only of destruction, and as parasitizing a dominant society and population that portrays itself as the font of true culture, ethics, society, and civilization. This is nothing new. The archetypal fascist politics of Nazi Germany used racial typology explicitly in this manner, drawing a stark line between "Aryans" and "Jews." As the Italian philosopher Simona Forti explores in her book *New Demons*, the "Aryan" was imagined as the apex of all racial types; tied historically to ancient Greece, it was the originator of culture, philosophy, art, and morality, a figure dedicated to the common good. By contrast, the "Jew" was imagined as manipulative and concerned with

84

personal gain, materialistic and exploitative where
the Aryan is spiritual and generous. Even more
than this, however, Forti explains that in Nazi
racial typology, the "Jew" was conceived not even
as an inferior racial group—which might come to
inhabit some lower rung in the racial order—but
closer to an absence of type altogether: as devoid
of soul or essence, lacking the power to create for
itself and destroying the fabric and foundation of
civilization. The "absence" the "Jew" embodied
here was not seen as something self-contained, but
as contagious—as having the capacity to spread
and thereby lead to the degeneration of the noble
"Aryan" and everything he had built. This philosophy laid the groundwork for genocide. By casting
its targets as not simply inferior or even inhuman,
but as embodying a threat to existence and essence
itself, it marked their exclusion and eradication as
part of the "common good."[1]

Nazi antisemitism is perhaps the closest
and most direct way in which demonization has
mirrored the frameworks of Christian demonology, demonstrating the dire consequences
it can lead to. Yet while contemporary fascist
politics can at times be more subtle, they often
channel the same core. In addition to the misap-
propriation of *taqiyyah* discussed before, it is,
for example, a common refrain in Islamophobic
circles that Muslims "love death" just as "we"
(that is, white, Christian Europeans) "love life."
Variations on this dichotomy can be found in
publications in French, Dutch, German, English,
and other languages, uttered by politicians,
journalists, academics, judges, and teachers.
Perhaps expectedly, it finds its greatest (albeit,
worryingly, not exclusive) presence among the far
right. In all cases, the language is tied to alleged
intrinsic differences between Muslims and (white,
Christian) Westerners, usually depicting the
latter as existentially threatened by the former,

the survival of the other requiring the death of
the self—the survival of Muslims (especially in
the West) being tantamount to the death of the
West. This dichotomy echoes the Nazi typology
of Aryan and Jew, aligning one side with life and
the other with death, one with futurity, prosperity,
and hope and the other with decline, decay, and
annihilation. The demonological themes are
important to stress here. Both Nazi antisemitism
and this strand of modern Islamophobia seek
to portray society as poised on the knife edge
between providence and perdition, between the
eternal life of the West and its damnation at the
hands of diabolical others who are denied the
capacity to do anything other than destroy.
	This current state of ascendant reactionary
politics and its fascist ideological accompaniments
has led to a climate of rampant and increasing
demonization, one which has sought to tarnish a
range of individuals and groups as threats to civilization itself. It has conjured demons, dredged up
from the long history of Christian Europe and its
traditional others, and crafted them anew for our
modern era. Yet for those of us who are marked
as being with these demons—whether afflicted by
them or affiliated to them—the question of what
is to be done remains. If we are to survive and
thrive in a society that increasingly demands our
exclusion or elimination—from public and political
life, if not from life itself—what politics must we
leverage, what bonds should we foster, what ties
should we seek to bind or to break? There are no
easy answers. The history of passing has taught
us that attempting to integrate into the structures
of dominant society offers one avenue of safety
and security. However, it also teaches us that this
route leads to profound alienation of the self and
is always subject to revocation. The passing subject
is always living on borrowed time. Even more, they
become the subject of demonization simply by

surviving. Their existence, and the means by which that existence has to be maintained in a world that would deny them, become the justification for their exposure and eradication. Yet if seeking to pass into and among the dominant systems of society can offer merely limited reprieve, what then?

A turn not simply to the history of passing but to its demonologies and demonization may offer potential insights for paths forward. The demonologies of passing I have discussed here accuse their targets of many things, but particularly of the inability to create, to found an original and authentic order. This accusation exposes cracks in the foundation that fascist politics seeks to reinforce. It ignores the reality that it has itself prevented those subjects it deems other from embodying their authenticities—or at least from doing so and still freely and openly participating in society. Fascist politics presents itself as the natural and eternal order of existence, while eliminating any possibility of alternative politics and—far more importantly—any people that it sees as embodying those alternatives and whose presence cannot be tolerated in its vision of paradise. Fascism demands that those it marks as unwelcome, like the devil in *Paradise Lost*, shift their forms to conform to the types of bodies and beliefs it allows within the walls of its garden, while also marking the people it contorts as threats to the garden's existence. Fascism claims that these people are inherently inauthentic, but also denies them the ability to be otherwise. It claims these people cannot build while demolishing anything they attempt to create. The intensity of this denial, and the violence it is enforced with, reveal that the fear at the heart of fascist politics is not simply that its others will tear down its perfect society, but that they may build something lasting in its place. That is, despite claims to the contrary, its devils can create—and not simply an imitation of

87

the existing social order but something new, filled with a legion of other forms of living that fascist politics cannot abide. In this denial, this demonization of alternative possibilities, fascist politics acknowledges a truth about itself that, in this era of its ascendance, those of us targeted by it—and not only us—would do well to acknowledge: for fascism to live, everyone else must die. If we are to survive, we must build a world not simply without it, but in which it has become impossible.

1   Simona Forti, *New Demons:
    Rethinking Power and Evil Today*,
    trans. Zakiya Hanafi (Stanford, CA:
    Stanford University Press, 2014).

Onset: Possession as Military Strategy

Anna Engelhardt and Mark Cinkevich

91

A demon roams through an ominous synthetic environment, reconstructed from satellite images of Russian air bases: Khmeimim in Syria, Baranovichi in Belarus, and Belbek in Ukraine. Passing through their deserted corridors, interrogation rooms, and electricity substations, this parasitic force sprawls out from the military structures. Devastation follows in its wake.

In *Onset* (2023), we craft an unholy alliance of medieval demonology, investigative research, and CGI animation to uncover the hidden life of these military outposts. Over the course of the film, the true horror of Russia's wars coalesces into a parasitic monster that possesses sovereign states and destroys them from within.

This text translates the film into two narrative strands, splitting the spreads of this book into two parts: the left half represents the film's voice-over narrative and intertitles, cowritten with and edited by Alex Quicho; the right half presents extensive open-source investigation, kept behind the scenes in the film itself. We advise the reader to start with the script. That way, when you read the research, it will reveal additional layers in the corresponding moments of the film. The illustrations are all stills, made in collaboration with Eduard Morocho-Baias, who oversaw CGI environments and virtual production.

Early morning. You're awake—not because of
a sudden noise that ruptures your sleep, but
because of a new and unusual quiet. Something's
not right. The nearby airport is still. No takeoffs
or landings roar between the horizon and sky. In
their place comes the sound of heavy vehicles,
distant voices, barking dogs. You strain to listen
to these changes, to begin to piece together
some context. From the window, all you can see
are shadows moving through the screen of the
night. Figures from the periphery swarm into
a shapeless mass. You take out your phone, hit
record, and zoom in.

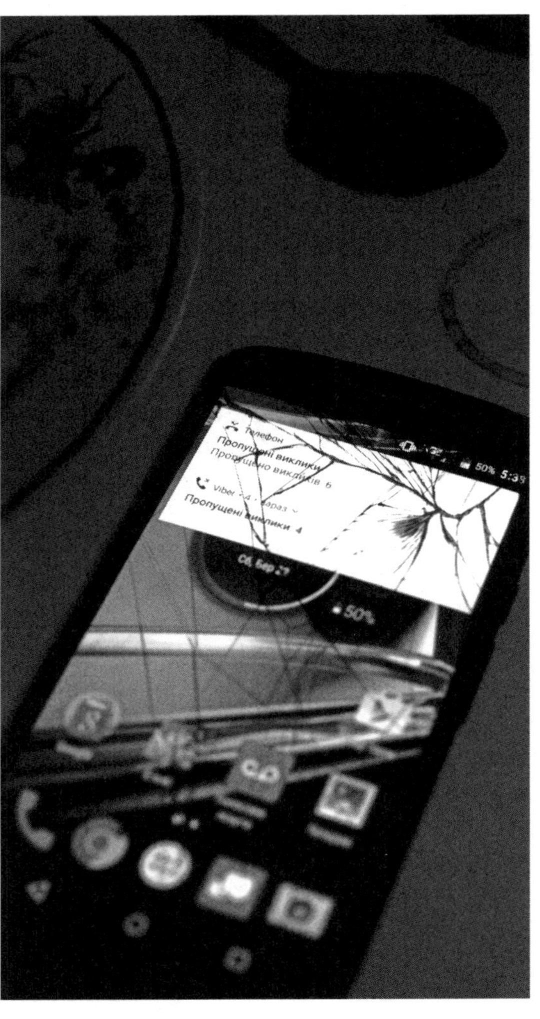

Military bases are often imagined as modern-day forts and castles—high-tech architectural projects specifically designed to serve the army. However, their reality is much more complex. Rather than being purpose-built, they are often converted from civilian airports and buildings taken over by Russian soldiers. One might say they are haunted by them—"appearing" as unannounced specters, Russian troops aim to invisibly transform an airport into a full-fledged air base. While preserving the facade of the structure, they corrupt its internal order. Remarkably, Russia consistently denies creating these air bases. This denial functions as a cloaking device, employed to blur the lines of invasion. It is a tactic that manifests in distinct but eerily consistent ways.

In 2020, the Russian military "appeared" at the Belarusian Baranavichy Air Base and has maintained a presence there since.[1] Russia never admitted it took over the base, instead concealing it as a military training center.[2] The Putin regime has been deploying jets and helicopters to the base under the guise of "training purposes," while the conversion was a quid pro quo for its support of the Lukashenko regime during nationwide protests.

In 2015, Russia remained reticent about establishing an air base in Syria. That year also saw the clandestine arrival of its soldiers at the Bassel al-Assad International Airport, a presence that the Russian government refuted. Contrasting with arrangements in Belarus, this foothold in Syria received legal status in 2017 through a forty-nine-year lease agreement, equipped with a clause for automatic extensions in twenty-five-year increments. The establishment of the Khmeimim Air Base can be considered a gesture of gratitude from the Assad regime, acknowledging Russia's significant role in supplying 85 percent of arms imports during the Syrian revolution.[3]

Location: Sevastopol International Airport (Crimea, Ukraine), renamed Russian Military Air Base Belbek after takeover by undercover Russian armed forces on March 22, 2014.

In 2014, shadows appeared at the edges of the airport in Crimea. Their faces were covered. Though they assumed humanlike forms, dressing their hulking bodies in plain clothing, they evaded civilian contact. They tried to remain undetectable through shape-shifting, replacing the darkness that the airport dispelled with its floodlighting and fluorescent interior. If you happened to ask a demon, "Who are you?" you would be met with two responses. One, with total silence. Two, with a deadly threat. They liked to punish those who dared approach them—and especially hated those who wanted to prove the demons' existence, the journalists and curious locals who arrived holding cameras and phones aloft. Hissing and cursing, they shut them down, mauling bodies and shattering lenses. Airport CCTV fell to the ground like birds dropping dead from a wire.

"The demon refuses to reveal itself, saying, 'If I tell thee my name, I bind not myself alone, but also the legion of demons under me.'" (The Testament of Solomon, *early medieval period. Author unknown*)

It is normal, instinctive to be terrified of demons. But do you know why they're dangerous? Open violence distracts from their true delight. They leap at the chance to offer false choices, and cut skewed deals just to enjoy the deception. As they swarmed the premises, the demons began to single out their prey from the airport personnel, choosing bodies ripe for possession. One by one, the people trapped inside the airport began to hear incantations. This was not divine intervention, delivering God's universal voice. The demons spoke to people, one by one, promising

A similar tactic was used by Russia during its annexation of Crimea. In 2014, the Ukrainian Sevastopol International Airport was taken over by Russian men in plain clothes, their faces concealed by balaclavas.[4] This form of invasion embodies the specific evil of silent interception—a form of possession. Its twisted logic unravels in two stages. Russian troops make their way inside the country unannounced. They hide their insignia, destroy any evidence of their presence, and create an appearance of unexplainable, almost paranormal interference. The deceptive logic goes: you cannot fight such a mysterious force with guns, and you will not realize that you can until it is too late. While unarmed Ukrainians were ready to resist, singing and marching against heavily armed Russian soldiers, they lacked the means to fight. The cruelty of this ghostlike occupation was that it depleted the Ukrainian resistance of weapons and military logistics and prevented an organized state response. Explicit aggression would have been no less difficult but more straightforward to repel than this insidious invasion.

This tactic runs deeper than the destruction of footage, evidence, and organized action. The mental state of the people who aim to resist is twisted and manipulated. When Russian forces took over Sevastopol International Airport, many Ukrainians were shocked that a significant number of their soldiers stationed in Crimea switched allegiance. However, this was not due to the weak character of those under occupation. Russian officers were sent to relentlessly seek meetings with the Ukrainian soldiers, cornering them one by one, lying that "[the Ukrainian government] will imprison you, initiate criminal cases against you."[5] Threats were exchanged for false promises of high salaries and housing. Russians were behaving like demons—not in the Catholic, grandiose meaning of a devil, but that of a Russian *bies*

personal benefits. They made enticing pledges of escape, supplies, or safe harbor—breaking individuals away from the collective, turning them against their kin. These promises left no traces, except in the involuntary reactions of those who listened. Their symptoms included lethargy, secrecy, and paranoid sweating as they surrendered to full possession. The demons broke and replaced their promises, intensifying and dashing feelings of hope, until their subjects lost touch with all reality—experiencing demonic visions instead.

"These possessed persons each had strange visions and fearful apparitions torment them inwardly, and hideous voices vexing them so extremely so they could feel no other pain or torture." (A True Discourse Concerning Possession and Dispossession, *1600. G. More*)

You wondered what could be happening. Much of the violence was invisible, an internal battle waged between host and parasite. From a distance, you longed to see them fight—for the release of confrontation, rather than the slow and secretive negotiation that depleted the spirit and drained resolve. At first, you could see some resistance: bands of people marching unarmed and fearless toward the demons, singing at the top of their lungs. Yet others opened the gates to the swarm. As the entities flowed in, bringing insidious darkness, the battle was lost before it even began.

According to Ukrainian colonel Yuliy Mamchur, only 38 percent of Ukrainian personnel stationed at the Sevastopol Airport escaped Russian occupation. Russian troops coerced many of the remainder into surrender.

or *chort*. A *bies* is a despicable minion of Satan, known to enjoy violence at any scale—in this case, from throwing rocks into jet engines to kidnapping and torturing people.

In these conditions, a Ukrainian soldier who succumbs is far from a deliberate traitor with malicious intent. The change in alliance is more similar to possession. In fact, possession bears many similarities to the Russian military tactic at large. Russian colonial specters haunt countries that successfully seek democratic change and independence. They perceive such change as a vulnerability—an opening for infiltrating the body of a nation, much like an evil spirit seeking to infest a host. Once it has appeared, the Russian army's colonial spirit aims to spread and take possession of an entire country from within. Possession, here, is not merely metaphorical—it is starkly literal. Infiltrating the sovereign body of a state, the army begins to hollow out and destroy it from within. Like demons, the invading forces penetrate the borders of a subject. They inhabit a body without permission, compelling it to act against its will and navigate material borders with a volatility that subverts the very demarcation of the self. In this way, invading forces, like spectral entities, have the capacity to fracture the ego of a nation, challenging its sense of identity and self-control. Thus, Russia does not merely occupy territories—it possesses them. It insinuates its control deep into the social and political body and, like a demon that knows no boundaries, begins its sinister governance.

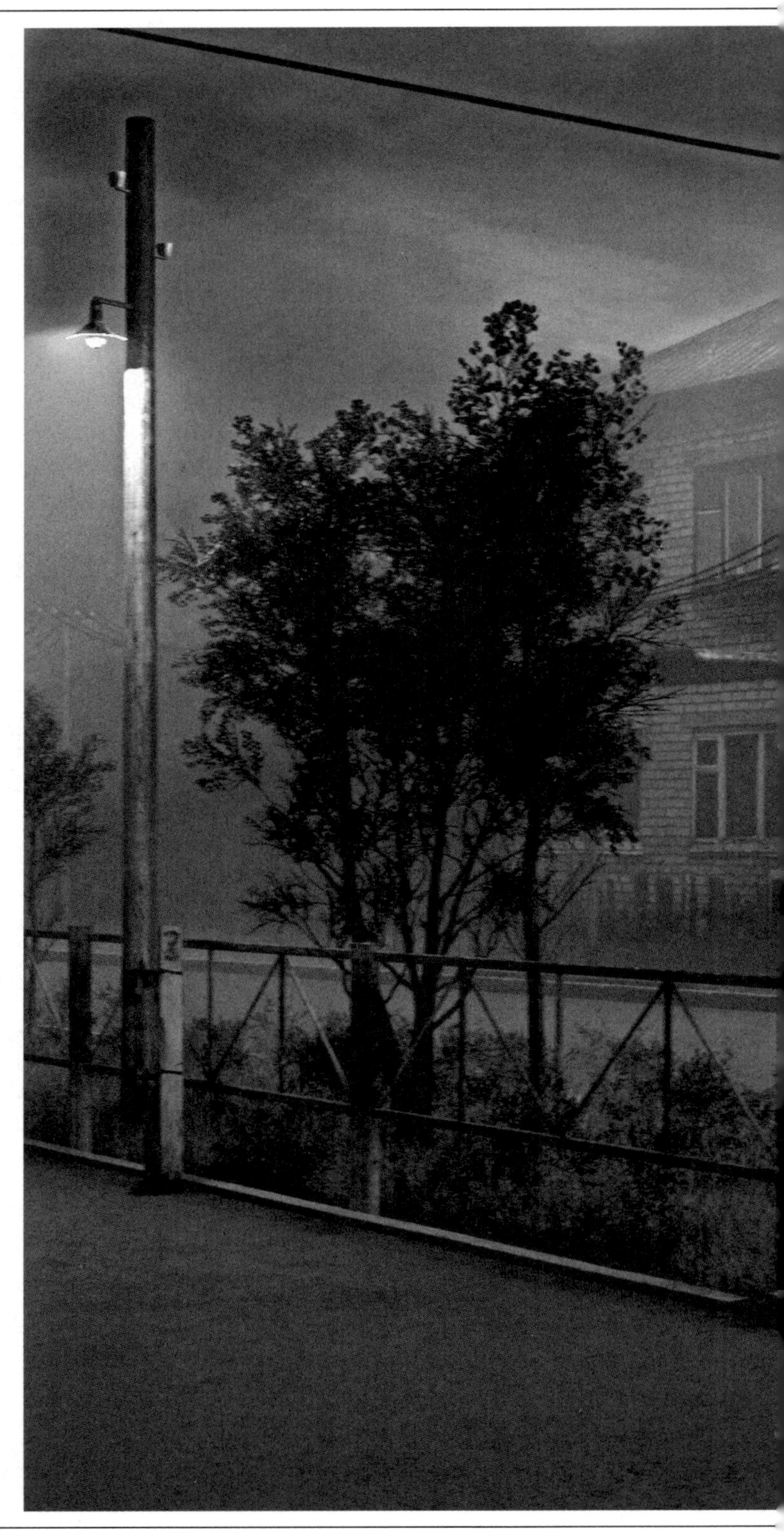

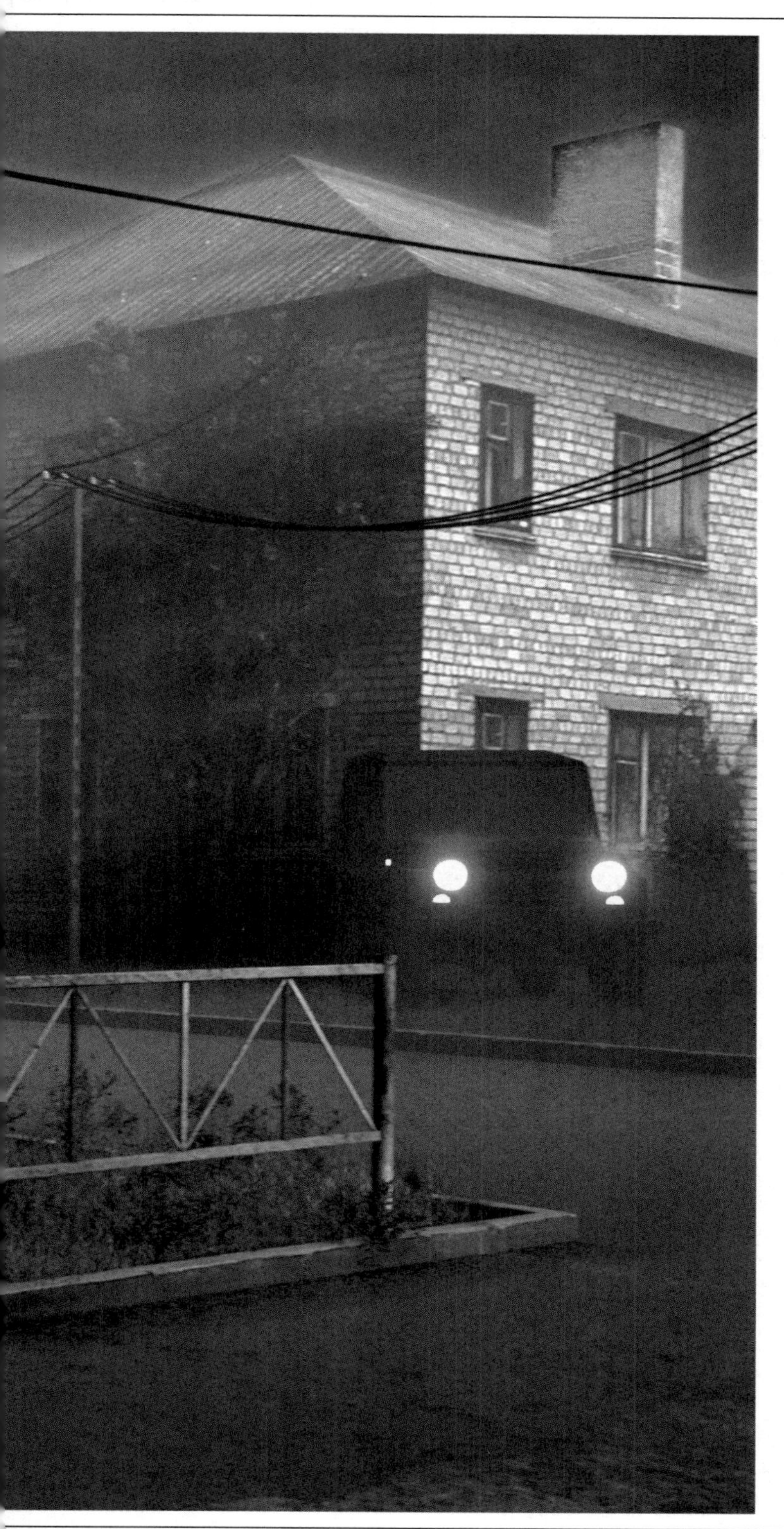

Location: Bassel al-Assad International Airport (Latakia, Syria), renamed Russian Military Air Base Khmeimim after takeover by undercover Russian armed forces in August 2015.

In 2015, the shadows appeared at the airport in Syria. The airport's previously healthy body, with its steady circulation of goods and equipment, suddenly succumbed to an infectious curse. Its belly, already full of crates and vehicles, began to swell to enormous proportions. Spaces meant for civilians were filled with weaponry, stuffed and stuffed with military equipment, cables, and pipes—until one morning brought relief in the form of destruction. A screaming filled the air, and a giant, distended bomber cut across the sky. Under the heavy airplane, the bloated airport burst. It started vomiting broken pieces of iron, cluster munitions, steel needles, white phosphorus, and shards of glass.[1] This mass, disgorged from the planes, rapidly spread the infestation. It tasted like metal and smelled like burning flesh.

"Vomiting foul objects indicates that the Devil has entered the victim's body. The discharge could include needles, hair, worms, or wax." (Memorable Histories, *1607. S. Goulart*)

Darkness clotted around the infected mass. It swept through the city as a rolling blackout, spreading to nearby houses, hospitals, and schools. The demons themselves were drawn to the glow of normal life—places rich with subjects to destroy or deceive. The ritual of devastation would begin. First, warplanes would vomit a deep shadow that concealed the advancing archdemons. Then, the rest would follow, drawn to the dark mass like flies to a corpse. The demons swarmed the hospitals, then lay in wait to prey on those who came to the rescue. The swarm spread through the schools, filled homes with rotten

A military base is not merely a concentration of soldiers; it is an intricate blend of infrastructure and manpower. While a collection of soldiers without infrastructure can be aptly termed a "military camp," it is the presence of these soldiers that transforms civilian facilities into military ones, defining their affiliation. A stark example of this is Russia's repurposing of the Bassel al-Assad International Airport. In September 2015, Russia transported fighter jets as well as attack and assault helicopters and started extending the existing infrastructure. The revamped airport boasted air-conditioned logistics containers, providing accommodation for one thousand people, a new air traffic control tower, extended runways, additional storage spaces, field kitchens, and refueling stations.[6]

However, Russia's narrative surrounding the establishment of the Khmeimim Air Base is riddled with denials and obfuscations. Initially, the takeover was outright denied. Then, as evidence of a deepening involvement became indisputable, a skewed narrative was presented. The Russian military often paints a picture of simply having "driven a stake in the middle of a field" to establish the base.[7] They conveniently ignore or downplay the existence of the Syrian airport. When mentioned, it's frequently described as an abandoned or dysfunctional facility by 2015, contrary to the truth.

This skewed portrayal allows Russia to argue that the air base, though it has civilian origins, is insulated, nestled within a protective "dome" in which any intruder would be eradicated. This starkly contrasts with the reality that the base is situated near several nonmilitarized urban areas. The blurred boundaries between military and civilian spheres compromise the base's autonomy, rendering dependence on civilian infrastructure a taboo subject. Energy sources in particular are veiled in secrecy. When asked about them, one military expert we consulted

darkness. It dreamed of total shadow—civilian normalcy disappeared with the light.

Launching from the captured Bassel al-Assad Airport, Russian-Assad air strikes targeted electricity infrastructure, leaving 70 percent of Syrian civilians without power.

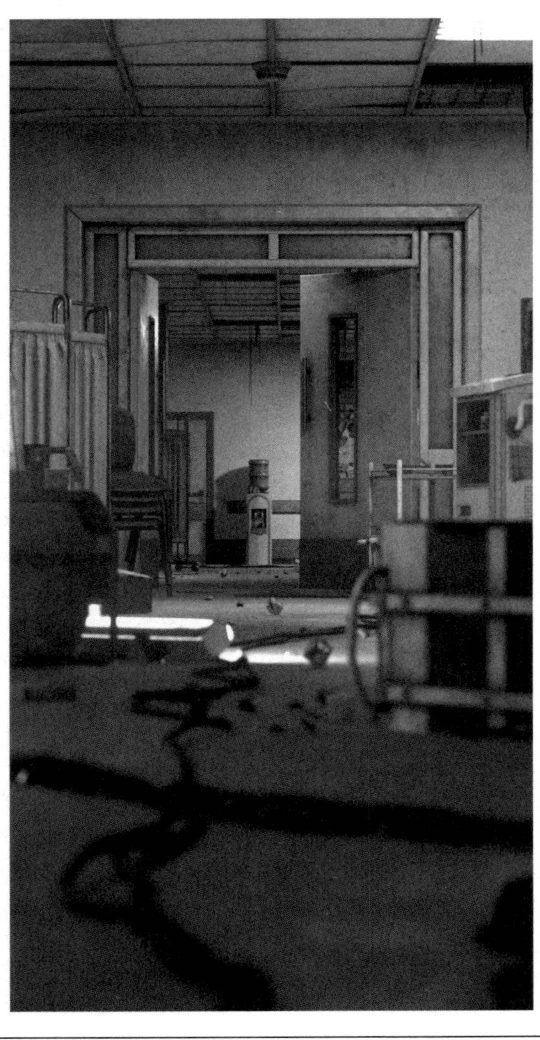

candidly admitted, "It's an interesting aspect I never considered."[8] In Russian there exists the phrase "To eat the Holy Spirit," which means to consume nothing. This aptly mirrors the obfuscation surrounding electricity consumption. While it is mentioned that bases rely on diesel or gasoline generators, the fact that these are merely stopgaps for civilian power interruptions is conveniently omitted. Publications on military electricity always look into the future, discussing the transition to autonomous energy sources, such as solar panels, while ignoring the present.

While exact figures for Russia remain elusive, it's noteworthy that the US Department of Defense is one of the world's foremost energy consumers. The Khmeimim Air Base, flaunted in Russian propaganda, exemplifies the nation's high-tech military prowess. To make it the single most well-known Russian base, numerous TV reports have been bragging about its air-conditioning and advanced medical equipment. Yet, the origin of the electricity that fuels it is never broached. The fact that the airport, before its militarization, relied on the civilian power grid—and remains tethered to it—is considered classified.

Such dependency should be viewed in tandem with the deliberate devastation of civilian infrastructure. This symbiotic relationship reveals a deep-seated malevolence, a calculated brutality epitomized by the notorious "double-tap" strikes, where Russian forces patiently wait for rescuers to arrive before launching a second assault on the same site.[9] Their meticulous plans for civilian infrastructure, charting a course of systematic obliteration—whether of schools, hospitals, or power grids—reveal an intent to cripple a nation. Yet, amid such orchestrated chaos, their own infrastructure remains untouched.

For instance, in 2017, when Syria grappled with crippling blackouts and a crumbling

The throes of the possessed, the bleeding and convulsions that wracked its body, drained it of vitality. For a time, its arteries were blocked; the blood that pumped through its veins grew still. But even as the demons gathered strength, hoarding resources and siphoning energy away from the living, they could not allow their host to die. They kept the country in a state of undeath, reanimating its infrastructure to circulate food, fuel, and energy. The body awoke to find its senses depleted, its will to live muffled by a singular, powerful hunger. It was only alive inasmuch as it was driven to relieve its possessor's insatiable appetite.

Terror is an energy-intensive state. A military base can use as much electricity as a steel plant—130 GWh per annum.

electricity infrastructure largely due to Russian bombardments, the Jableh substation—linked to the air base—was renovated.[10] Its capacity increased by a thousand times, even as countless Syrian regions languished in darkness. Simultaneously, all other Russian electricity projects in the country were realized, keeping only its military bases illuminated. Russian troops are well aware that electricity means power without which people, Syrian civilians in this case, are vulnerable to attacks. This principle was coldly articulated by a Russian military pilot in Syria who had witnessed or even carried out attacks on the power grid himself: "It is easy to say where I should fly [to drop bombs] during the night. Where there is light—there is peace. Where there is no light—there are terrorists."[11]

Location: Baranavichy Military Air Base (Brest, Belarus), renamed Russian Military Air Base Baranovichi after takeover by undercover Russian armed forces on September 22, 2020.

In 2020, the demons came for Belarus. Shadows emerged at the air base and made their way inside the country to devour it from the inside out. Delirium had taken hold of the state's body, its vital systems suffocated by new, crazed habits. The demons toggled with power at the source, bringing down darkness at unpredictable moments, choking out services before restoring moments of seeming normalcy. The possessed state, unwittingly losing control over itself, began to experience the demons' thoughts and desires as its own. Internal organs shifted in secret, rerouting energy flows and changing the country's constitution. Power lines were felled or diverted, turning the country into prey. The shadows were crafting a new system, enveloping themselves in a network of pumping vessels to fuel the destruction ravaging the country: a kind of autocannibalism, the body turning in to feed on itself.

Russian manipulation of energy infrastructure in Belarus was most apparent in cities built to serve power plants. In areas forced to reduce production, substations would often fall into decay and spontaneously catch fire.

You wake up with a start. You're in your room. It's dark. You reach over to turn on the light. Was it all just a bad dream? Flipping the switch makes no difference. Nightmare and reality have become one and the same. You turn to the open window for air and notice how apparent the feeding is at night. The airport has remained luminous long after sunset, piercing through the deep gloom that has been forced over the entire country. The glow, hypnotic and dim, is protected by a braid of cords grown to grotesque proportions.

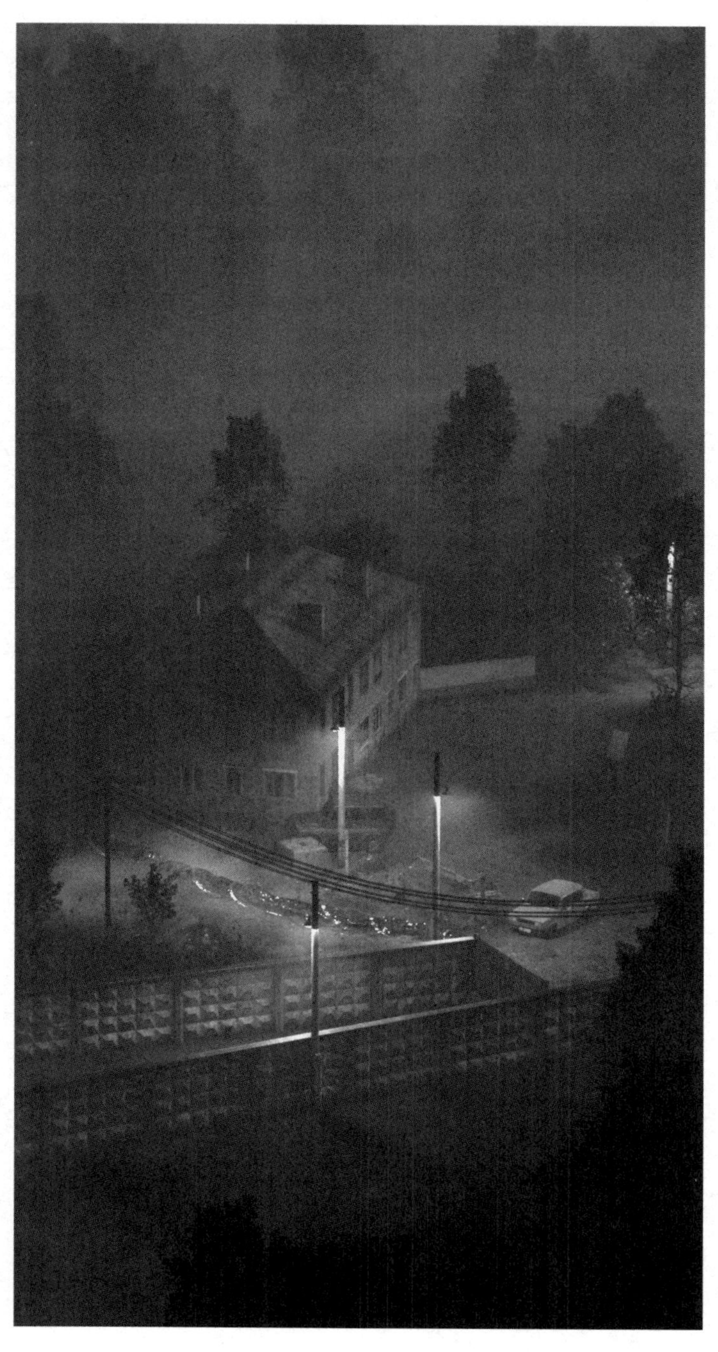

These make up an umbilical cord, swollen with the energy that feeds into the airport. The cables bonding host and demon are carefully concealed yet detectable on the ground. The energy they transmit is volatile, so they cannot stretch far. In fact, you can reach the source on foot.

The demon holds a victim between its claws, ready to devour the lost soul. It disinters cadavers and eats them, leaving nothing behind except bones. (Dictionnaire Infernal, 1818. J. A. S. Collin de Plancy, M.-C. Delmas)

You leave the house and walk, not toward the airport but away from it, using the great tangle of wires as a navigational guide. Be aware of where you came from and where you are going to. Do not make any noise. Listen to the pulsating hum deep within the wires. Find the rhythm and directions in which it drains and sustains the host. You will find yourself entering territory that exists only as a gray zone on the map. You will have to remember every step you take deeper into the zone, because nothing else will guide your return. If you are traveling at night, a hostile metallic buzz will alert you to the fact that you're approaching the source. At dusk or sunrise, it will be the sudden sight of shadows, long and sinister, that will signal that you've arrived. From a short distance, the structure looks familiar, an everyday power plant not unlike the one installed in a neglected quadrant of your town. Still, it doesn't quite match up to its surroundings. It is not out of place, but rather, out of proportion. It has grown so much that it has become uncanny—unrecognizable.

Russian occupying forces repeatedly expanded the electricity substation of Baranavichy Military Air Base until they reached the limit of its technical capability.

Mirroring the visceral and consuming relationship of demonic possession, Russia's takeover of Belarusian air bases, particularly Baranovichi, represents an insidious form of control. Just as a demon, once embedded within the host, draws upon the vital energies that sustain it, so too does Russia sustain its presence within the Belarusian infrastructure by feeding upon it. Here, the lifeblood is not of a supernatural order. It is electricity, the nervous system of a modern nation-state, pulsing through substations and wires, animating both the mundane and the extraordinary aspects of contemporary life, including the military apparatus.

Electricity is not just a utility; it is a means of wielding control and projecting power. The missiles that launch from Baranovichi Air Base, the jets that are repaired in the adjacent aviation plant—all of this requires a stable, high-volume flow of energy. This is vividly illustrated by the extensive renovations of the substation supplying the base and repair plant. In 2020, it was upgraded with a sophisticated protection system against explosions and fires. The advanced safety monitoring clearly reflects its strategic value. This was no mere facility update but a stark amplification of the military's demonic grip.[12]

Russia's engagement with the broader Belarusian electric infrastructure has also been marked by a more disruptive approach. Reports of new Russian-controlled mega-infrastructures, which come at the expense of systematic freezing and the destruction of the existing power grid, show a force that is not just occupying but actively consuming its host. While the substations supplying the bases are renewed every year to meet the growing energy consumption of the Russian military, the Belarusian energy production is scaled down to make space for Russian-sponsored energy projects, such as a nuclear power plant in Astravets.[13]

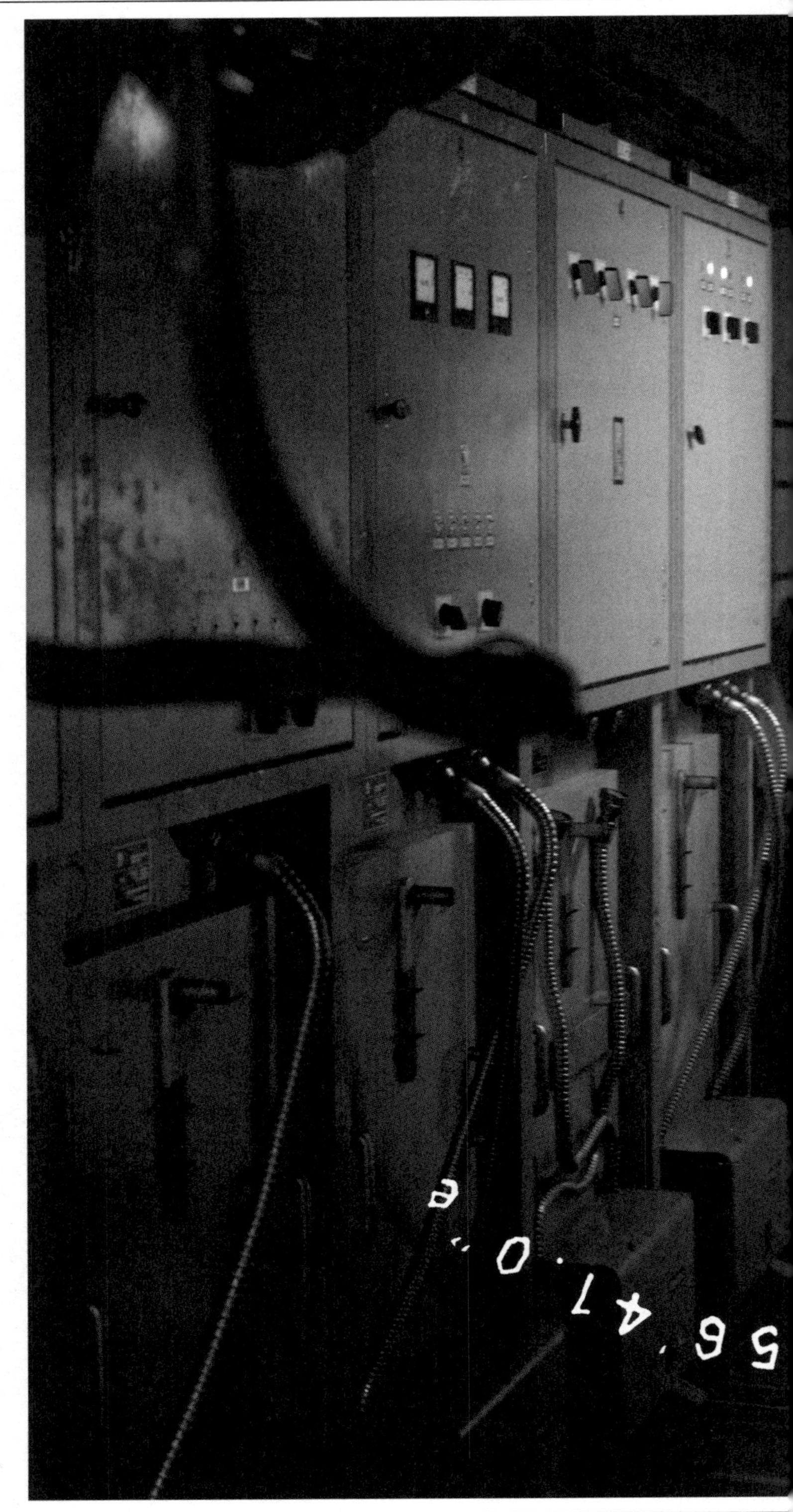

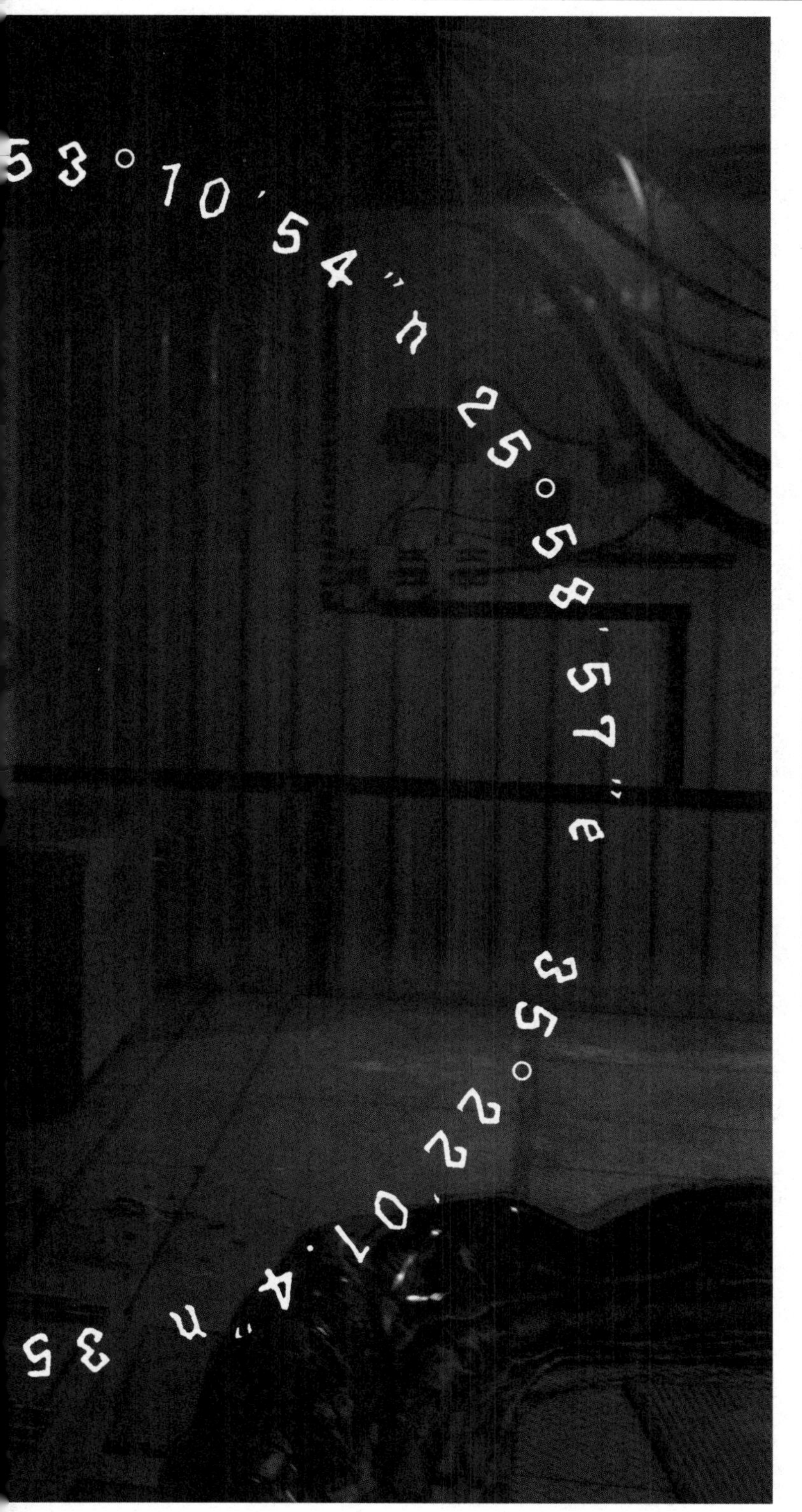
53°10'54"n 25°58'57"e 35°22'07"n 35°

The monstrous thing before you smells of ozone.
Your head is heavy, and the air is so charged it's
hard to take a breath. Your thoughts materialize
as blurs, fragmented and deformed. Do you recall
why you are here? Look closely at this organ,
with its cryptic cords and wires. Search for the
numbers that it stands upon. Write them down. Its
coordinates should form a circle. The organism
that formed it will go within it. It is the demon.

*Victims can seek protection from a demon
by drawing a seal—a diagram of the demon's
true name: "Having the Seal of the Spirit
required . . . to preserve thee from danger,
and also to command the Spirits by." (Ars
Goetia, 17th century. Author unknown)*

Close your eyes and retrace your steps. How
many did it take you to walk the umbilical cord?
Strip your path of all hesitant twists and turns,
the self-doubt that caused you to double back.
Now, it should form one line within the circle.

Your trail closes the loop. The seal is complete,
luring the demon into its endless border.

Do you remember the onset of possession? It's
hardly possible to capture it all in one image.
Too many instances, events, and occupations
haunt your mind now. Yet through the blur comes
the certainty that you can name it. At last, you
can call it by its true name.

Russia obtained control over Belarus to
the extent of enmeshing it into its power grid.
The initial takeover, focused largely on seizing
energy pipelines and cords, set the stage
for the subsequent military occupation. To
command a country's energy is, in many ways,
to hold its destiny. The military occupation,
then, is but a logical continuation of the initial
energy-focused one.

In this context, possession is more than
control. It is a form of autocannibalism—a
consuming from within, where the parasite does
not merely subjugate the host but reshapes it,
repurposes it, and, in some ways, devours it. The
assumed autonomy of the Baranovichi Air Base,
in this light, starkly illustrates the depth and
intimacy of this possession. It stands as a material
manifestation of how energy infrastructure, in
the hands of a dominating power, can become
both a weapon and a form of binding—an umbilical cord that nourishes the occupier while slowly
draining the life force of the occupied.

The air base operates seemingly autonomously, under the guise of a self-contained,
self-sustaining military installation. Yet, this
autonomy is illusory. The military base is tied
to the neighboring substation. The specifics of
electricity as a resource—its volatility, its need
for high-voltage transmission infrastructure, its
resistance to long-distance transport without
significant loss—mandate proximity between
the parasite and host.

This exposes these highly secretive military
substations. Using open-source intelligence tools
such as Google Earth Pro, one can locate them.
To map them is to map the vulnerabilities of the
Russian occupation.[14]

1 International Campaign to Ban Landmines – Cluster Munition Coalition, *Cluster Munition Monitor 2016*, 2016, http://www.the-monitor.org/media/2394895/Cluster-Munition-Monitor-2016-Web.pdf.

Onset (2023)

Film by Anna Engelhardt and Mark Cinkevich
Written by Anna Engelhardt, Mark Cinkevich, and Alex Quicho
Story editor: Alex Quicho
CGI environments & virtual production: Eduard Morocho-Baias
Soundtrack: Yikii Tong
Voice-over actor: J. E. Burton
Underscore: Regular Citizen
Sound designer & engineer: Alisa Kibin

Funded by Transmediale, Pro Helvetia, and Henie Onstad Kunstsenter

1   Georgiy Filin, "Rossiya perebrosila voyennuyu tekhniku v BLR" [Russia transferred military equipment to Belarus], *Nasha Versia*, October 5, 2023, https://versia.ru/rossiya-skrytno-perebrosila-v-belorussiyu-voennyx-i-texniku.

2   Vladimir Dorokhov, "V chem sut' voyennogo sotrudnichestva Belarusi i Rossii?" [What is the essence of military cooperation between Belarus and Russia?], Deutsche Welle, March 22, 2021, https://www.dw.com/ru/uchebnyj-centr-ili-aviabaza-v-chem-sut-voennogo-sotrudnichestva-rb-i-rf/a-56933524.

3   Alexandra Kuimova, "Russia's Arms Transfers to the MENA Region," *EuroMeSCo Policy Brief*, April 1, 2019, https://www.euromesco.net/wp-content/uploads/2019/03/Brief95-Russia-Arms-transfer-to-the-MENA-region.pdf.

4   "Russian Troops Storm Ukrainian Bases in Crimea," BBC News, March 22, 2014, https://www.bbc.com/news/world-europe-26698754.

5   Yuliy Mamchur, "Yuliy Mamchur: My videli eshche v Bel'beke, Krymom eto vse ne zakonchitsya" [Yuliy Mamchur: We saw it in Belbek, Crimea won't be the end], interview by Mariya Semenchenko et al., Argument, July 30, 2014, https://argumentua.com/stati/yulii-mamchur-my-videli-eshche-v-belbeke-krymom-eto-vse-ne-zakonchitsya. All translations are our own.

6   Anna Maria Dyner, "Three Months of Russian Intervention in Syria: The Military and Political Implications," *PISM Bulletin*, January 8, 2016, https://www.pism.pl/upload/images/artykuly/legacy/files/21212.pdf.

7   "'My zdes' nadolgo': vo chto Rossiya prevratila svoyu bazu v Sirii" ["We are here for the long haul": What Russia has turned its base in Syria into], RIA Novosti, August 27, 2020, https://ria.ru/20200827/siriya-1576338369.html.

8   Siarhei Bohdan, "On the Infrastructures of Military Bases," interview by Anna Engelhardt and Mark Cinkevich, 2022.

9   Syria Justice and Accountability Centre, *When the Planes Return: Double-Tap Strikes on Civilians in Syria*, July 2022, https://syriaaccountability.org/content/files/2022/08/English-Double-Tap-1.pdf.

10 Fuad Alhaj Omar et al., "The Effect of the Syrian Crisis on Electricity Supply and the Household Life in North-West Syria: A University-Based Study," *Education and Conflict Review* 3 (2023): 77–86.

11 "Voyennaya priyemka. Aviatsiya v Sirii. Samolety. Chast' 2" [Military reception point. Aviation in Syria. Airplanes. Part 2], Zvezda TV, August 14, 2017, video, 36:25, https://youtu.be/wd-WffhESBA.

12 "Na podstantsii 330 kV 'Baranovichi' ispytan i vvedën v ekspluatatsiyu avtotransformator" [At the 330 kV "Baranovichi" substation, the autotransformer has been tested and put into operation], Brestenergo, August 5, 2020, https://www.brestenergo.by/Новость/326.

13 Anna Engelhardt and Mark Cinkevich, "Imperial Power Grid: The Role of Energy in Russia's Colonial Expansion," Le Club de Mediapart, April 8, 2022, https://blogs.mediapart.fr/berliner-gazette/blog/080422/imperial-power-grid-role-energy-russia-s-colonial-expansion.

14 Anna Engelhardt and Mark Cinkevich, "Onset ÷ Applied Demonology," Transmediale, February 28, 2023, video, 27:06, https://youtu.be/F7qlTdM1pxM.

Putinist Russia and the World's Fascist Moment

Ilya Budraitskis

119

We can define the world's current state as a "fascist moment." It is not only a matter of the growing support for the far right in Europe and Latin America, the rise of Chinese authoritarianism, and the doings of the Putin regime as it pursues its criminal war in Ukraine. Fascistization, as a complex combination of the rationale of state apparatuses, the dynamics of political movements, and popular psychology, represents the breakout of a tendency immanent to market-based society as a whole.

Fascism has not reemerged in the historical guise we know from the first half of the 20th century. It has not been "reborn" because it is, by definition, devoid of historical continuity and has never constituted a coherent ideological project. On the contrary, fascism thrives by aestheticizing history, by arbitrarily extracting narratives and images to suit the needs of the current political imaginary. Historicism, as an idea that envisions the world's progress toward a better future, is all the more alien to it. Fascism does not stem from an obligatory or desirable state of affairs but from a real state of affairs, which is constantly replicated because human nature, rooted in ruthless struggle and the desire for domination, remains unchanged. Like a century ago, today's fascist moment totalizes these maxims of economic behavior, extending them to politics, society, and international relations. States and cultures, like individuals, are imagined as locked in a permanent conflict replicated over time.

According to the official Putinist narrative, Russia has been confronting the aggressive West for centuries, and "Russia's great culture" has been one of the key weapons in this struggle. Ukraine, in this conception, has no independent essence; it is an artificial project, an "anti-Russia" (as Vladimir Putin defines it), whose only raison d'être is to act as "the West's battering ram" in its project of destroying Russia.[1] There is nothing new about this story, and

121

every event only reprises the hoary archetype. Time loops in an "eternal return" in which individual and collective agency is nullified, thus asserting destiny's absolute power over human beings.

World War II Didn't Happen?

This temporal regime maps the "disappearance of a sense of history" in postmodern "late capitalism," which Fredric Jameson once described. Analyzing the workings of popular culture, he showed that its consumption, rooted in the severing of all connections among images extracted from different contexts and eras, resembles a schizophrenic's sensibility. "Our entire contemporary social system," Jameson wrote, "has little by little begun to lose its capacity to retain its own past, has begun to live in a perpetual present and in a perpetual change that obliterates traditions of the kind which all earlier social formations have had in one way or another to preserve."[2] Jameson's conclusion was prompted by the situation in the early 1990s, when the universal dissemination of neoliberalism's unconstrained market principles was echoed by claims about the "end of history." In today's geopolitical "clash of civilizations," each with its own unchanging "essence," we are witnessing the true end of history as an idea of emergence in which nothing is perennial and there is always another future on the horizon to redefine and dismantle the existing order. In this sense, the two competing explanations of the world after the fall of the Berlin Wall—Francis Fukuyama's and Samuel P. Huntington's[3]—have been synthesized, and the end product is the end of history as an endless clash of civilizations.

This absence of history functions by displacing from the collective memory events that had fundamentally divided time into a "before" and an "after," events in whose wake the world, its notions and values, could no longer be the same. The

122

current fascist moment has put paid to two such events previously defining the historical meaning of the 20th century: the Russian Revolution of 1917 and World War II. While the first event reminded us that the oppressed can radically alter their circumstances and their "destiny" on their own, the second one told us that we should never repeat the monstrous experience of global war.

The effort to make sense of World War II generated the entire set of moral ideas and international institutions on which, all reservations aside, the contemporary world, or, more precisely, our sense of "normality," was until recently built. Even radical critiques of this order of things invoked a set of concepts drawing on the lessons taught by World War II: the unconditional condemnation of military aggression, universal human rights, and the inadmissibility of all forms of racism. This critique was grounded in "normality," since it revealed the inconsistencies between realpolitik and the world order's generally accepted norms. The West's military interventions in Afghanistan and Iraq, which were in fact acts of aggression, were camouflaged with "humanitarian" declarations, or explained away as acts of self-defense. They were (to borrow Hannah Arendt's expression) "old-fashioned moral crimes," or simple hypocrisy, which did not seek to establish new norms but played fast and loose with the old ones.[4]

Russia's invasion of Ukraine effected a genuine break with normality by rejecting this vocabulary of familiar concepts. Without positing a new universal language, Putin's Russia has proposed something more serious—making absolute relativism the new norm by constantly redefining concepts from a position of strength. The notion of a "multipolar world," championed by the Kremlin, is based on the idea that moral and historical arguments are not grounded in a common language but reducible to mere attributes of a particular

123

state's power. The "disappearance of a sense of history," mentioned above, is no longer expressed in a pop-cultural play on dehistoricized images but as part and parcel of state ideology. For example, official Russian propaganda actually dubs all its enemies, foreign and domestic, "fascists," while "anti-fascism" is declared a part of the distinct Russian identity. Moreover, Putin's ideological narrative portrays the invasion of Ukraine as a replay of World War II, with Russian "anti-fascists" confronting a "fascist" West. The memory of a war that should never be repeated is thus turned into its opposite: we remember the heroic deeds of that war to repeat them over and over again. "1941–45: we can do it again" is the succinct wording on the patriotic stickers that, in recent years, millions of Russians have pasted on their cars during the annual May 9 Victory Day celebrations.

A Process without a Subject

"Fascism" and "anti-fascism" have thus become synonymous with the duo of "friend" and "enemy," which, in keeping with Carl Schmitt's notorious definition, forms the basis of politics. For Schmitt, this meant that moral and legal concepts have no independent regulative meaning and are constantly redefined through conflict. The true source of law—the decision-making sovereign—punches through the empty husk of norms, he argued.[5] This enabled him to justify Adolf Hitler's 1934 massive extrajudicial liquidation of political opponents, known as the Night of the Long Knives. By transcending the rule of law, Schmitt argued, we can arrive at a political answer (*who* should decide the matter) rather than a moral answer (*how* the matter should be decided).

In today's fascist moment, however, the sovereign does not make history but affirms his allegiance to the archetype. When justifying the necessity of launching the so-called special military operation in February 2022, Putin insisted that his hand had been forced. He had "no other choice": he was only obeying fate, succumbing to the perennially rehashed showdown between Russia and the West, which figures as a kind of Althusserian "process without a subject."[6]

This paradoxical combination of voluntarism and fatalism reveals the profound link between contemporary fascism and neoliberal expediency. The neoliberal subject acknowledges the impossibility of altering the circumstances that dictate its will, but simultaneously it acts as a decider, constantly choosing the best behavior under conditions over which it has no power. Each of its particular decisions is thus a way of evading a genuine decision and recognizing the impossibility of achieving maximum arbitrariness, absolute "sovereignty." Nonstop action is the market agent's modus operandi: it must constantly react to circumstances and accept reality as a multitude of external challenges. Reality appears to it as something unknowable and chaotic, devoid of internal coherence and direction.

The capitalist individual's efforts are rational vis-à-vis the irrational whole. Such irrationalism in private life is at odds with liberal democracy, which presupposes a kind of overall consensus about the rationality of everything that occurs. The complete loss of this horizon of reasonability—that is, of the notion (however vague) of a common interest and the progressive growth of a collective morality—extends fatalism to politics. Fascistization means nothing less than the emergence of market individualism as the logic of the state.

The world has been turned into an arena of ruthless competition not only among different centers of power but also among particularistic, homogeneous mindsets. In his multivolume work *Noomakhia*, Alexander Dugin, the Putinist state's most flamboyant and consistent ideologue, has

125

hatched an entire theory of the *logos* of various civilizations.[7] Each civilization, according to him, has a unique archetypal mentality, its own worldview, which is ahistorical in nature and unconsciously reproduced over the millennia. For example, there is, he alleges, a direct link between the rituals of the Celtic Druids and Lacanian psychoanalysis due to the existence of a "French *logos*." Chinese foreign policy and the peculiarities of the political regime in India also heed the particular mindsets of their civilizations, whose main features are immutable. Consciousness is neither universal in nature nor in a state of becoming; rather, it constantly repeats the same moves within its particular civilization. Dugin fancies himself a Platonist, yet this boils down to the claim that ideas are eternal and immovable—although they do not have the quality of absolute truth, because the Russian "truth" never overlaps with the Japanese or the Arabic truth, for example. The supreme spiritual values, which the state enjoins its citizens to adopt, mean obeying the collective destiny without questioning.

Thus, in early 2023, the Russian government announced the launch of DNA of Russia, a large-scale program of school and university courses. Tellingly, DNA in this case stands for "spiritual and moral culture" (*dukhovno-nravstennaia kul'tura*, or DNK, the Russian initialism for DNA), directly equating biology with culture. One of the main courses, Fundamentals of Russian Statehood—compulsory in all tertiary institutions—tasks itself with "bridging the gap between a person's actual identity and the realization of that identity."[8] Unconscious affiliation, as expressed in language and behavioral norms, should become a conscious matter, thus taking on the quality of a holistic system. This memory of obligation continues to be present biologically, as it were, but has been temporarily displaced

126

from the minds of most young people, who are still under the influence of a hostile Western culture. With a little coercion from the state, their cultural "DNA" is activated, and they find themselves by recalling their predestination.

Culture is conceived here as an innate property tasked with defending the nation as a unified body, with fortifying it in the face of competition from other cultures (which are practically different biological species). Such fidelity to biology, which harmonizes the corporal and the mental, is simultaneously the best investment in oneself. As the course syllabus argues, a nation is "human capital," constantly growing as it "realizes its identity."[9] Tellingly, the tendency toward the self-growth of capital in this approach corresponds to a fixed state of consciousness identical to its civilizational archetype.

This is an extreme instance of what György Lukacs defined as the "reification of consciousness"—that is, consciousness adopting the commodity form, the transformation of the individual into a commodity among other commodities.[10] "Human capital" (a concept borrowed directly from neoliberal jargon) refers to the supreme reduction of the human being to the commodity form's abstraction. Individuals who have an identical mindset equated with their biological unity (previously identified as racial unity in the Hitlerian version of fascism) are transformed into the capital possessed by the state qua civilization. The state thus becomes a form of capital, its direct expression. Fascism involves overcoming and destroying the political institutions and civil rights that mediate the relationship between the individual and the state and prevent the unlimited disposition of people as capital.

Fascism as the power of abstraction is paradoxically not at odds with fascist contempt for
"abstract" human rights and international law.
Even early 19th-century conservatives criticized
the Enlightenment and the French Revolution as a
triumph of abstract principles derived from pure
reason and not based on historical experience.
As Joseph de Maistre wrote, "In my lifetime I
have seen Frenchmen, Italians, Russians, etc. . . .
But as for man, I declare that I have never in my
life met him."[11] The abstract man created by the
Enlightenment is devoid of the original form passed
down from ancestors and inherited in cultural and
state traditions (i.e., the "cultural code," as Russian
propaganda defines it nowadays). This person has
inalienable rights, since it belongs to humanity as a
single community, and therefore affirms universal-
ism as a principle. At the same time, the universal
recognition of the individual gives it freedom of
choice, including its own identity.

Fascist racism is directed against those who
stand as embodied abstractions, who rebel against
traditional forms. Secularized Jews, with their
passion for universalist ideas, or Slavs, as agents
of anti-state bolshevism, have symbolized this
formlessness at various times among fascists.[12] As
they saw it, the forces of chaos were concentrated
in their primary foe, the organized working class,
with its allegiance to the ideas of social equality
and international solidarity. Fear of the shapeless,
animated by fleeting emotions and the rootless
masses, has generally played a key role in all fascist
movements.[13] The revival of caste hierarchy, in which
everyone knows their place and heeds their natural
destiny, remains in one form or another fascism's
primary project, its image of the desired future.

In their propaganda, today's ultrarightists
have predominantly replaced "abstract man" with

Muslims, as disenfranchised migrants or alleged adherents of a global caliphate, as well as with LGBT people, who challenge gender norms. In Putin's Russia, which acts as the vanguard of the global fascist moment, any public expression of LGBT identity is a criminal offense, and gender reassignment is completely prohibited. Russians must be specific in their affiliations, and their place in life by fact of birth must be firmly established in the hierarchy of social forms. The state, in keeping with Putin's apt slogan, is the apex of this patriarchal hierarchy, a "family of families" united under the paternal authority of the nation's leader. The "collective West," as the bearer of universalist liberalism, with its principles of human rights and freedom of individual choice, has been proclaimed Russia's principal foe. The object of hatred is "global liberal elites" who destroy "traditional values," foremost those of the West itself. Over the heads of these hidden elites, with their secret plans of creating a "mechanical man" (Sergey Naryshkin) liberated from its true natural essence,[14] Putin's Russia stands in solidarity with all the conservative forces of the Western world. The Kremlin's support for Donald Trump and Marine Le Pen is thus not opportunistic but ideological and programmatic.

Rooted in the Russian reactionary tradition, criticism of the West is paradoxically combined with Eurocentrism. Like in the 19th century, in today's Russian political imaginary, the collective West is the only real entity from which imperial Russia demands recognition as an equal. Putin's "anti-colonial" rhetoric and publicly stated "pivot to the East" should not fool us: they are merely the levers Russia needs to eventually take its rightful place among the dominant European nations. To achieve this goal, Russia must return the West to its true spiritual foundations and force it to recollect its traditions. More recently, amid the ongoing war in Ukraine, Vladislav Surkov, one of the Kremlin's

129

ideologues, published a provocative article predicting the future creation of a "Great North," an equal triune alliance of Russia, the United States, and Europe that would dominate the world. The road to this alliance would be long, Surkov argued, but it was inevitable because of the common messianic Roman legacy of its members.[15]

Empire and Imperialism

The notion that empire is Russia's "destiny," the only possible form of its existence, has been one of the key tenets of Putin's official ideology. In the Russian conservative paradigm (most vividly mapped in the 19th century by Konstantin Leontiev), the imperial form was defined as existing outside of time: unlike modern nation-states, the empire does not strive for perfection and equality, but instead preserves the "blossoming multitude" of endless class and cultural differences from being swallowed up by history. The burden of empire, Leontiev argued, was to resist progress and preserve a timeless equilibrium of differences. This immobility of empire as a form, however, has always created a need for the mobilization of its borders. To remain unchanging, the empire must constantly push outward, expanding its territory. It is this permanent outward expansion, as Surkov wrote in an earlier article, that helps maintain political stability by "exporting chaos" and "accumulating new lands."[16]

The archaic idea of empire in this interpretation jibes completely with imperialism, a phenomenon of the modern age and the capitalist system. Rosa Luxemburg argued that imperialism was predetermined by the very structure of capital accumulation, which constantly has to surpass its limits and expropriate territories and economic patterns not yet plugged into the capitalist economy.[17] In *The Origins of Totalitarianism*, Hannah Arendt developed this line of thought,

arguing that imperialism was a direct precursor
to European fascism.[18] In her view, imperialism
replaced the political idea of the state as a community based on consensus with the economic rationale of continuous expansion. Imperialism did not
involve enlarging the boundaries of the political
community; on the contrary, it established an
impenetrable border between the metropolis and
the colonies. Political power, which had previously
been tasked with preventing violence at home,
instrumentalized uncontrolled violence beyond its
borders. The identity of power and violence laid
down by European imperialism then returned to
the heart of Europe in the guise of deportations
and death camps. The mass extermination and
dehumanization of subjugated populations
practiced by the colonizers were unleashed by the
totalitarian state on the home front.

Imperialism thus both affirms the insurmount-
able borders between the foreign and the domestic
and makes them movable and contingent. Russian
imperialist expansion in Ukraine, beginning in
2014, was marked by the creation of fictitious
"people's republics" that were fully dependent on
Moscow, but whose legal regimes were markedly
different. Whereas Putinist Russia was, until 2022,
an authoritarian regime that resorted only to
targeted crackdowns, the violence of the armed
groups affiliated with the local leaders in Donetsk
and Luhansk was virtually unrestricted. Once the
full-scale invasion of Ukraine commenced, the
Russian regime's transformation into a straightforward brutal dictatorship was largely embodied
by the export of this culture of violence from the
hinterlands to the imperial center.

**The Fascist Moment as the Fullness
of Contemporaneity**

At the global level, Russia, as a semiperipheral
region, became neoliberal capitalism's "weak

link" and was the first to realize its latent tendency toward fascistization. This tendency, combining the tension between inside and outside I have described, is both an acceleration of neoliberal capitalism and a quasi-critique of it. The anti-Western ressentiment that is one of the main motifs of Putinist propaganda often includes a critique of "radical neoliberalism" in which the particular "collectivism" of the Russian people is contrasted with Western "individualism."[19] In a similar vein, European right-wing populists denounce "globalist elites" who are destroying the established lifeways of ordinary people. However, fascism in the first half of the 20th century was even more radical: it directly attacked "plutocratic capitalism," offering an alternative in the guise of a corporate "people's community" that would surmount class conflicts.

Today's fascist moment has emerged from the neoliberal "perpetual present" and differs from classical fascism in its complete lack of a utopian horizon, however reactionary. Just like a century ago, however, fascism has been born out of capitalism's nonsynchronicity, the coexistence of different experiences of time within the same reality. As Ernst Bloch has shown, German Nazism was the means by which intermediate social groups that did not fit into modernity—whose worldviews were seemingly "backward" vis-à-vis their own era—could enter the political arena.[20] Nevertheless, this "backwardness" is not only a legitimate part of a complexly organized contemporaneity, but also proves capable of taking command of its internal, previously hidden tendencies.

In our day, the far right, with its calls to "bring back" the bygone harmony of the nation-state, is both a reaction to neoliberal capitalism's contra-dictions and an expression of its mainstream. Our contingent "contemporaneity" manifests itself in its entirety insofar as it brings to light everything

132

that was previously displaced, everything that was recently treated as archaic and a relic of the past.

Two decades ago, the liberal Western mainstream deemed the right-wing critique of globalization as a threat to national sovereignty a powerless attempt to stop the advent of a future in which there would be no barriers to the free movement of goods and people. Today, we can state that neoliberal globalization has proved to be a necessary stage on the road to deglobalization and the extension of the logic of market competition to the level of states in a marvelous new "multipolar world." Post-Soviet Russia, which was the testing ground for radical market reforms in the 1990s, then, has synthesized the ultimate neoliberal expediency and its reactionary, anti-liberal ideology in the form of a neofascist regime. This regime does not offer the world an alternative project or open the horizon to a shared, albeit frightening, future. On the contrary, it is entirely rooted in the present as an "endless horror show," acting as the concentration of the world's fascist moment.

Translated from the Russian by Thomas H. Campbell

133

1 Vladimir Putin, "On the Historical Unity of Russians and Ukrainians," President of Russia, July 12, 2021, http://en.kremlin.ru/events/president/news/66181. Unless otherwise noted, all translations are by Thomas H. Campbell.

2 Fredric Jameson, "Postmodernism and Consumer Society," in *The Cultural Turn: Selected Writings on the Postmodern, 1983–1998* (London: Verso, 1998), 1–20, here 20.

3 Francis Fukuyama, *The End of History and the Last Man* (New York: Free Press, 1992); Samuel P. Huntington, *The Clash of Civilizations* (New York: Simon & Schuster, 1996).

4 Hannah Arendt, "Some Questions of Moral Philosophy," *Social Research* 61, no. 4 (1994): 739–64, here 743.

5 Carl Schmitt, *The Concept of the Political*, trans. George Schwab (Chicago: The University of Chicago Press, 1996).

6 Louis Althusser, "Reply to John Lewis," in *Essays in Self-Criticism*, trans. Grahame Locke (London: New Left Books, 1976), 33–99, here 56.

7 "'Noomakhia': Wars of the Mind," Eurasianist Internet Archive, accessed January 22, 2024, https://eurasianist-archive.com/menu/noomakhia-wars-of-the-mind/.

8 "DNK Rossii" [DNA of Russia], Russian Presidential Academy of National Economy and Public Administration, accessed February 7, 2024, https://firo.ranepa.ru/dna-of-russia.

9 Ibid.

10 György Lukács, "Reification and the Consciousness of the Proletariat," in *History and Class Consciousness*, trans. Rodney Livingstone (Cambridge, MA: MIT Press, 1971), 83–222.

11 Joseph de Maistre, *Considerations on France*, trans. Richard A. Lebrun (Cambridge: Cambridge University Press, 1994), 53.

12 Carl Schmitt, *Roman Catholicism and Political Form*, trans. G. L. Ulmen (Westport, CT: Praeger, 1996).

13 Ishay Landa, *Fascism and the Masses: The Revolt against the Last Humans, 1848–1945* (New York: Routledge, 2018).

14 "Naryshkin zayavil, chto zdorovomu cheloveku 'poroy strashno priyezzhat' v Evropu'" [Naryshkin said it is "sometimes scary for a healthy person to come to Europe"], TASS, August 25, 2023, https://tass.ru/moskovskaya-konferenciya-po-bezopasnosti/18513299.

15 Vladislav Surkov, "Rozhdeniye Severa" [The birth of the North], Aktual'nyye kommentarii, September 27, 2023, https://actualcomment.ru/rozhdenie-severa-2309262036.html.

16 Vladislav Surkov, "Kuda delsya khaos? Raspakovka stabil'nosti" [Where has the chaos gone? Unpacking stability], Aktual'nyye kommentarii, November 20, 2021, https://actualcomment.ru/kuda-delsya-khaos-raspakovka-stabilnosti-2111201336.html.

17 Rosa Luxemburg, *The Accumulation of Capital*, trans. Agnes Schwarzschild (London: Routledge, 2003).

18 Hannah Arendt, *The Origins of Totalitarianism* (Cleveland, OH: Meridian, 1962), 124.

19 "Putin raskritikoval 'radikal'iyy neoliberalism'" [Putin criticizes "radical neoliberalism"], TASS, August 24, 2023, https://tass.ru/politika/18576329.

20 Ernst Bloch, *The Heritage of Our Times*, trans. Neville and Stephen Plaice (Cambridge, UK: Polity, 2009).

Five Easy Pieces for Little German[1]

Roman Osminkin

139

We are political émigrés from Petersburg. Germany gave us a humanitarian visa. We were placed in the village of Thräna, in the municipality of Borna in Saxony's Leipzig district. We live well. You could say we lucked out: because we have a small child, we were given a separate studio flat, rather than being assigned to a *Heim* or a refugee camp, although accessing public transport is complicated.

I have come to love our trips with German, aka Gerochka, to the nearest grocery store, which is a four-kilometer walk from our house. Nastya started classes at the Academy in Leipzig, and three times a week Gerochka and I are alone from morning till evening. (Nastya paints my eyebrows black, since, over the last year, they have lost the black-browedness I inherited from my mother, a native of Zhitomir.) I also like our weekly trips to the store so much because they are our only so-called public outings. German and I walk through the fields of Saxony, sheep grazing on the right, white swans nibbling the grass on the left, and we dissolve into the politics of the landscape. For Gerochka, time does not yet exist—it is infinite. For me, time as *chronos* no longer exists. It has become an emotionally transfigured end-time that has redefined all my previous daily affairs and things in an eschatological perspective.

The wind is always blowing in the field. Sometimes it is intoxicated with the scents of wildflowers, sometimes with freshly spread manure, sometimes with a moist foretaste of the coming rain. The weather in the field can change several times during the hour our trip takes: the clouds overhead float very quickly, casting bizarre shadows on the ground. When it starts to rain, Gerochka and I ask it to stop, and if the rain is in a good mood, it stops quickly. Lyosha Grinbaum once wrote to me that we would feel like we belonged in this land when German said his first word in German.

141

The local Hannah Arendts often ride past and smile at us discreetly, saying *Hallo*. A little less frequently, Heidegger rides by on his bicycle, his thin lips clenched. He nods slightly and sometimes even looks away, as if he knows we know that he didn't apologize to Celan during their only encounter. Recently, we passed a German man recklessly wielding a chainsaw on his property. Pumped, tattooed, and handsome, the fortysomething was chopping a mountain of trunks into short discs (a substitute for Russian hydrocarbons?) while wearing headphones. He was the spitting image of Barthes's woodcutter, who not only chops wood but has something to say about it. Or rather he was probably listening to Schelling's lectures on natural philosophy, realizing his unity with the tree, as if he were one of its branches that had stood on its own two feet and awakened the consciousness slumbering in the tree amid the latest spiral of nature's dialectical evolution.

A father pushing a child in a stroller is not exactly a rarity in Germany, but social acceptance has its own aura. The saleswomen at the supermarket already recognize Gerochka and smile and wink at me. However, there is no touching as there is among Turkish people, but rather a distanced German warmth, and from especially elderly women there is just tenderness and a few extra minutes in life. The teenage girls like to drink different drinks in the entrance of the supermarket and make funny faces at German every time, while I pretend to be in control of the situation, rolling the grocery cart and German's stroller before me.

Gerochka behaves quite indecently at the supermarket. As if a little shopaholic devil has possessed him, he tries to grab from the shelf anything within reach of his hands, shrieking and laughing ecstatically. Either the number of multicolored, motley attractors exceeds a critical mass for him, or he gets bored because of my slow progress, which is due to the fact that I often have to aim my smartphone at this or that product to translate its name and ingredients using Google Translate. One time German was grunting and straining until he was red in the face and doing it so loudly the entire supermarket could hear him. I was scared, thinking he was pooping. I don't take diapers and wipes with me to the supermarket because babies poop very rarely when seated, or rather they almost never poop. But German was straining so loudly that the Germans—hand it to their courtesy—averted their eyes understandingly.

There aren't many things that divide our lives into before and after, and almost all of them have been described as liminal or transitional, as becoming "other" through some kind of initiation ritual. There are things related to external historical events, like war and emigration. But having a child divides your life into before and after not only in terms of social practices; it's a kind of emotional experience that reshapes you from the inside out and never lets you go back to your old self again. Now you are never alone; your life is not yours alone. It has been a year and three months, but I cannot, even when I'm out walking without German, not think about him, about how he's doing. It's as if a little other is now permanently settled in your heart, and this isn't a metaphor: it literally lives in your body, and you are responsible for it. I don't know how long this will last, but what matters is learning to maintain the delicate balance between the constant anxiety for this little creature inside you and the joy of belonging to each other.

On the way back, I feed Gerochka sugar- and salt-free corn puffs, so he won't get cranky. When we get home, I take off my wet T-shirt and collapse on the mattress, waiting for my feet to stop burning, and Gerochka crawls over me and comically tucks himself under my armpit, as if realizing that Daddy is tired and needs to lie down

143

for five minutes. At these moments, I am almost happy. I will not explain why I am *almost* happy, because this sketch is not about fucking up your mood even worse.

Walking and babysitting a baby, you experience unique moments that our career-oriented society considers wasted time. But can caring for a new person be called wasted time? Below, you will read a few plays that grew out of conversations with my partner Anastasia Vepreva and our joint experience of parenthood and emigration.

1. It's Not That Clear-Cut

Check it out. The baby pooped.

It's not that clear-cut.

I'm telling you: it smells like shit.

I'm not sure. I don't have sufficient grounds to think it happened.

Just smell it!

I don't think it's a matter of trial and error.

No, look, it's definitely shit.

That's positivism, but the smell of shit is the smell of life.

Wipe his ass.

Let's make do without imperatives.

Where's the syringe? The baby's got snot in his nose.

Maybe it's just drool or other secretions that don't pose a threat and don't require violent extradition.

You're messing with me while he's crying and can't breathe through his nose.

Oh yes, but it's more complicated than that. Pacifier and diaper, spoon and blanket, washing and buttons: a baby's world is reflected in thousands of everyday little things.

He's got yellow fucking mucus in his nose.

It's a weird color, somewhere between canary yellow and olive green, I'd say.

We have to suck it out. Where's the syringe?

Why do you ask me that? My paternal identity is not 100 percent of my identity as a person.

Okay, it's time for the baby to eat. He's begging for food.

Are you sure? There are different ways of interpreting his request. And is it a request at all, rather than a simple extralinguistic paraverbal gesture of pure pleasure on the part of a being who has not yet incorporated language and communicates with the world via the full range of its psychosomatic machinery?

Look how hungry he is, how he's devouring his food.

Yes, I guess he is eating eagerly, but that doesn't mean anything, because a good appetite can be caused by various things, including the reemergence of displaced needs.

Did you just fart, or was it German?

I wouldn't permit myself to fart out loud.

Are you kidding?

Of course not, for if I farted out loud, it would mean that my bodily nether regions had outgunned my spiritual upper reaches, that *physis* had torn the crap out of *logos*, and next time I wouldn't fart, but—

The baby wants to sleep. He's rubbing his eyes and falling over. Can you rock him?

Rocking is not just translational and rotational motion, but a new loop of the eternal return, because the lullaby ritornello is being playing at becoming.

That's it. He's throwing a tantrum!

I wouldn't jump to conclusions . . .

(And so on.)

R. comes onstage and says: I look at the Syrian women sitting on the street barefoot with their babies. They have nothing, but they are smiling. And immediately I think, They get by okay.

A chorus of grandmothers runs onstage and says: But back in our day there were no antibiotics, no diapers, no washing machines. Basically, women gave birth in the fields and didn't complain, but look at how spoiled they are nowadays. Technology does the work for them, and they shamelessly still have the gall to complain.

Then a chorus of great-grandmothers runs onstage and says: Oh, they feel sorry for their children. Back in our day, God gaveth and God taketh away without any abortions and contraceptives. If women had a dozen children at once, they wouldn't sweat it. Maybe a couple of them would survive, and the rest would be God's will.

Then Tatar-Mongols run onstage and say: Oh, look how the Slavs have multiplied through the rafters! We'll enslave you. We'll take your wives into captivity. We'll massacre your little children. Submit to us, bend your head under our yoke, and you'll live.

And then dinosaurs come bounding onstage: thump, thump, thump … mmmm … aaaaah … thump, thump, thump, thump … mmmm …

Following all this, R. comes out again and says: No really, that's how little people need in this life. They get by okay.

A. comes onstage and says: You have just seen a play illustrating anachronism, a device by which our feelings and actions are deliberately projected onto another historical period, thereby supposedly making us feel guilty and ashamed of our own psychological instability.

3. Fines in the Mail

Oh look, they put our last names on our mailbox! That's so cute!

It's to make it easier to send fines by mail.

Gerochka crawls so funny! He bangs his knees on the floor.

If the neighbors downstairs hear it, the fine will come in the mail.

Oh, I think I got the garbage and food waste containers mixed up.

That's it! Now we're going to get a fine in the mail.

I forgot to turn off the torrent. What happens now?

We'll get a fine in the mail.

Oh, look at the swans! How they nibble on the grass! I wonder if you can take pictures of them.

The fine will arrive in the mail.

Look, what a beautiful snowdrop! Let's dig it up and plant it at home in a milk carton!

The fine will arrive in the mail.

On the trail to the lake there's a sign in three languages, including Russian, saying you can't fish, otherwise—

Otherwise, you'll get a fine in the mail.

Oh, please translate what it says on the poster with the pooping dog.

It says: Pick up your canine's *Kacke* or—

You'll get a fine in the mail?

Not quite. Or have your canine do its *Kacken* at home.

Oh, that's passive aggression.

No, no, Germans are quite polite, especially in small towns. Everyone says hello to each other, but if you don't say hello—

You'll get a fine in the mail?

No, you'll be considered a cad, a bad sort.

Oh, I think I forgot to say hello to the tomcat in the window.

147

Gee, I wondered why the cat looked at us like we were shit.

Maybe he's just a snob.

Or maybe he knows there's already a fine in our mailbox.

4. Beat Yourself Up

Oh, I diced the carrot into triangles, not cubes, and German is throwing a fit.

Beat yourself up.

Do you know what we're called?

Emigrants? Relocatees? Refugees?

No, real refugees live in tents and have it bad. We're just *exiles*.

Beat yourself up.

I don't think we're doing enough for the triumph of good over evil. Why do others volunteer from morning till night, and we don't?

Beat yourself up.

We abandoned our home although no one was bombing it. Maybe we were cowards and should have gone to prison like Navalny and Skochilenko.

Beat yourself up.

I think we're bad parents because we don't spend enough time raising our son.

By not enough time you mean twenty-three hours a day instead of twenty-four? Beat yourself up.

Don't exaggerate, you know what I'm talking about: books on child-rearing by Komarovsky and Katasonov, educational games, counting the calories and micronutrients in the baby's diet, medical checkups and vaccinations—

Beat yourself up like there's no tomorrow!

Keep your voice down, or the Germans will hear us talking and realize we're from Russia.

They'll beat us up.

148

Sometimes I don't know whether
it's my hypertrophied sense of guilt or
self-victimization. It's like a bipolar swing.
Just beat yourself up and you'll understand.
Like the NCO's widow?
Close. Like an SMO widow.
I'm eating this cheesecake and I'm—
Beating yourself up.
I don't think we're *weird* enough.
Beat yourself up.
Actually, flagellation is a common practice
in BDSM, and BDSM is closer to *weird*.
There you go.
Why do I always play the good cop while
you play the bad cop?
Because you like beating yourself up.
Do you like beating other people up?
No, I just know there's no such thing as a
good cop.

5. Small Talks

A: I sent applications to three kindergartens,
but then I felt sad, because I don't want to
send German to kindergarten.
R: Oh yes, we've gotten so used to having
Gerochka at home, and he's used to us.
It's been over a year. How will he get on
without us?
A: But then he refused to eat, and I changed
my mind.

A: The duck book lasted ninety minutes.
R: How's that? What do we do now?
A: Now we have to read three duck
books to him.

A: Germany switched to daylight saving
time today.
R: Does that mean the difference between us
and Russia is now an hour less?

149

A: No, Roma, the difference between you and
    Russia will only increase.

R: You didn't listen to classical music when you
    were pregnant and now our son is anxious.
A: Not necessarily. The local newspaper,
    Sächsische Zeitung, polled its readers about
    whether operas should be rewritten. After all,
    by today's standards, nearly all operas in the
    repertoire are sexist, racist, jingoistic, or all
    of the above.

A: They gave us jars for getting samples of the
    baby's urine and feces too. We can scrape
    the feces from his diaper, but how can we get
    a sample of his urine? Google says there is
    some kind of "urine collector" for that.
R: The word *urine collector* sounds poetic.
    I remember that Krivulin called the
    boiler plants where the underground
    poets and artists of Leningrad worked
    "warmth-creation cellars," meaning cellars
    where heat was generated.
A: A urine collector is this special bag you tape
    to a particular place on the child's body. And
    you get a sample of his urine with ease.
R: With ease, indeed . . . You know, I just
    massaged his prostate, and he peed in the jar.
A: Well done, but we just got a call from an
    official saying that our interpreter made a
    mistake and instead of urine we should have
    collected two jars of feces.

A: I constantly want to get new toys for
    German, but it's like I want to get them
    for me too. I dreamed of getting a Lego set
    as a kid, but there were only those Soviet
    constructor sets. Although they were cool,
    too. They were so metallic.

150

R:	Everything in the Soviet Union was metallic, even my father's teeth after he did two stints in prison. I still remember how they clattered when he would open a beer with them.

A *(monologue)*: More and more often, Instagram shows me videos along the lines of, I got up at five in the morning, made myself breakfast, did my makeup, and went jogging, then I cleaned up, made breakfast, lunch, and dinner for my husband and our seven children, then I did aerobics and dance, then my husband and children woke up, I fed all of them, changed everything, then I went to the gym with the kids, then I painted and meditated, then I fed everyone again, then I played educational games with the kids … Just watching this video wears me out.

Translated from the Russian by Thomas H. Campbell

151

1   German (the Russian version of
    the name Herman) is the name
    of the artist Anastasia Vepreva's
    and my son. We named our son
    before the Great War and our
    emigration to Germany. We can
    put it down to fate or quote the
    old Soviet cartoon *Adventures of
    Captain Wrongel*: "As you name
    a ship, so shall it sail." But there is
    another thing: when we moved
    to Germany, we realized how
    ambivalent the name was. When
    we are asked our son's name in
    Germany, as happens, and we
    reply that it is German, people
    think at first that we are identifying
    his nationality as German.
    Wondering why Russian parents
    have a German son, they then nod
    and ask again, okay, your son is
    German, but what is his name?

The Streets Are Visible (Excerpt)

Franziska Füchsl

157

I have a child today. Whether I'll still have it
tomorrow, I can't say. It could end up being taken
from me, it could slip my grasp, escape, run away.
It could get snatched up. But today, today I have
one. And you should enjoy the things you have as
long as they're around.

Today's the day I realized that two always
belong to every window: the view out and the view
in, my curiosity from up here down out below and
the curiosity from down there up here, over here
from over there or even from the floors above
me into my space down here. It never occurred
to me that someone could possibly want to know
something about me. Still though, the quietest
movement of the eyes can be an intruder.

As of today's date, I have a daughter. I reported
her and they officially certified her. A funny
daughter, a daughter with guts. She's out playing
in the neighborhood with order and tracking
numbers in her hands and her mother's name and
address on the tip of her tongue. She's well looked
after. Such a blessing that everyone's curious,
everyone's looking after her. We're all looking
after us. The only thing missing is the father in a
crocodile button-down.

I'm a victim. That's also been officially certified.
Marks fill the headers and footers, the reference
number. My family, in which I am the only
member—as far as I know—has a caseworker who's
an inspector. It follows from the witness testimony
UP_1 suspicion of: FRAUD (oZoo1) to the detriment
of the party: ME in addition to UP_2 suspicion of:
FRAUD (oZoo2) to the detriment of the party: ME.

We speak German—I declined the need for
an interpreter. From the transcript of the hearing,
I learned how to spell the word *Dolmetsch*. If
the inspector hadn't complimented me on my
command of German, I could have continued
on with my antics in searching for a partner so
that I could provide a couple as my answer to the

question of my relationship to a third party. As it is, I concede—ultimately, the gift of inspection belongs to his position. I let him click the appropriate answer: I emphatically deny any relationship to a third party. That is, single, a single mother, throwing a glance at my inspector.

My official status: victim/claimant. I prefer claimant; I'm fond of titles ending in -ant. Just call the damage by its name. The fact that I am a claimant, though, shouldn't have any sort of negative impact on my motherhood. In this case it appears to be more of an honor, or at the very least a rectification. It probably has something to do with the following remark: the claim itself is not proof that such events have in fact taken place. The confirmation that I am a claimant, just as the confirmation that ostensibly affirms my motherhood, doesn't appear to have any characteristics of factual witness testimony as would pertain to my general witnessing capacity as a mother. The charge has been filed under the abovementioned reference number. Charge, as if I had already gotten something back that had been previously purchased—my daughter, for instance, or an "unknown perpetrator."

There seem to be competing terms on my daughter's birth certificate: act alternating with incident. I prefer incident. Her birth somehow nearly slipped my mind, ME: I then contacted customer service via email and let them know that I hadn't placed an order. Customer service informed me that the order was placed under the customer ID: "Person: defendant, last name: UP_1, sex: female, role: fraudulently attained goods." I don't even have a customer account.

I then see that I forgot my signature. Will this have an impact on my witness status?

My neighbor—the bearer of happy customers—told me that he had spoken to the postman, who he has recognized for a while now, after he had just delivered the second package ordered under my name—since he himself was waiting for a package delivery at that moment.

Type: shoes (other)
Description: Air Max LTD 3, Nike
LiBi: no
Recovered: no
Other attributes: pair

The information leaflet "victim information leaflet" was delivered.
The information leaflet "victim emergency line_new easy read format LL B1" was delivered.
0800112112.
You can call us every day.
You can call us twenty-four hours a day.
You can also write us an email or use our chatbot.
You don't need to tell us your name.
You don't need to pay anything.
You have these rights and in some cases these rights too, and you may even be eligible to entitlements.

Type: clothing (other)
Description: Lacoste T-shirt
LiBi: no
Recovered: no
Other attributes: white

The declarations/notices/explanations were signed by the witness. Version 18.01.2018.
I should give her a name.
The package delivery man, who's incorrectly termed "postman" in the official documents, verified that the girl in question was able to extensively provide information pertaining to the identity of her mother. But what about my willingness to be that mother? An official report always

requires two parties. And why didn't the package delivery man ask the security question? Why didn't my carrier—who I still don't recognize—ask that brat who her father is?

And what's your father's name, little girl?

"Mailman"—the crafty little thing would have answered—I mean, she's my daughter after all. And bursting out laughing the postman would have turned his face upward, and his face would have flown past my window, the mother's window—and like every good mother I sit at home waiting for my Hermes, for his heavy steps climbing the stairs. Waiting an eternity in the doorway, all by my lonesome, frozen. He didn't even send my daughter up to me. Is my delivery man the one flitting around the streets on little Nike wings?

The postman asked my neighbor if he knew me and if I had a daughter. Mr. Neighbor kindly let the postman know that I did not have a daughter. Upon hearing this, the postman made clear that on his way to the claimant—at the corner where the two streets meet—he was intercepted by a woman. This woman had the order confirmation and the tracking number. Ergo: he handed over the package to her.

I've already adopted many women. When they're out on the streets trying to get some fresh air, wailing like hyenas, and our fine little neighborhood passes right over them, instead of addressing them directly, I gladly offer an open ear and bits of advice. With a mixture of tissues, wine, and questions, I keep them afloat; they don't even notice that I'm their prompter. But then something always runs awry: and in the end they'll slink back to their lions, who have been combing the area looking for them, growling and belling, up and down the streets in their slick whips. They're crying, our men—the hyenas think—and then—they fall into my arms and: thank you, thank you, there! Just before they run out in front of the car, get in, and

162

roar into a certain future alongside their lions' glistening manes. To be honest, something's calling me home too. Lost daughters.

Such a blessing that questioning is subject to a weak conjugation: the questioner, the official bureaucrat, Mr. Inspector. The questioned, the person, the claimant. We've entered into an especially conjugal relationship. The questioning inspector and the questionably depraved ant. The beauty and the eager to please.

Such a blessing that to do harm is subject to a strong conjugation: she who did the damages, the unknown perpetrator. And she who does the talking and is done for, claimant, mother, me. From one to the other, it can happen fast. With a slight smile, I let the inspector know that my relationship to my daughter—who will one day grow up to be a woman like myself—is of the strong inflection. I have on lipstick, to make sure I'm questioned properly. And while his lips continuously lurk in an annoyingly silly e-scape, mine quill and stretch, quill and stretch between O and Mmm, O-Mmm.

Response: I have not experienced any concrete material damages.

Response: I had the opportunity to look through this protocol page by page (pages: 1), or to allow it to be examined by an interpreter or my third-party representative.

Response: I had the opportunity to inflect the corrections properly.

Response: I did not inflict any changes.

Such a blessing that inflicting something is subject to a strong inflection. Between the lips' silly e-scape and O-Mmm, the attempt to maintain calm, the relationships, i-e i-e, are unquestionable and deafening.

I was informed of my right to refuse testimony in the case against members of my own family. Response: I am a legal adult and take part in this case as a private party. In doing so, I explicitly

163

relinquish my right to refuse testimony against members of my own family and would like to testify. The hunt for my daughter has begun. The matter now rests upon a desk.

I make my way out into the street and with every passing woman and little girl ask myself if she could be my daughter. Now I know how parents with children feel, who can't escape moaning about how they cost them dearly. They outgrow cuddling, they start testing your nerves and put you on probation. I'd really like to go through with this case against my daughter because she never once clung to me. You know what, I'll bring this case if only as a response to the complete absence of any physical embrace! And on top of that, one should testify against such a child as long as everything is still fresh.

I emerge out on the street. Where did those times go, when children still loved to love?

My neighbor, the package delivery man, and I have a child. You could also say: our neighborhood has a child. My neighbor and I have yet to meet this child face-to-face, but the postman, who is a true bearer, would recognize her. Apparently, he's seen our daughter run away from him a few times. Next time, he'll try to snap a quick photo.

I still haven't had the chance to discuss this whole matter with our delivery man in private—but not because I don't want to have anything to do with him; we're separated, people just go their separate ways. Honestly, I've never even spoken with the delivery man, just the two of us. Pretty unusual for a daily relationship that functions smoothly and seems to avoid any kind of scandal. We meet each other indirectly: at the newly installed yellow boxes, at the mailbox, and in the form of my neighbor. We haven't met directly at the door in ages, and if we ever have, then it was definitely pretty loose, in the form of two faces relegated to the files.

164

Just like it should be for parents, I'm worried about our daughter. And just like it should be for a mailman, my neighbor assures me that he, too, is worried sick. His care for me takes the form of my mailbox, my packages—it takes place in the language of delivery. Right now, he still trusts my neighbor with my orders, but he'll soon recognize that I place my orders with none other than him. At some point he'll finally give in to his curiosity to look me in the eye just as an item is passed between us—and every day I eagerly await a message from my Sir Inspector.

Hark! What's that I hear coming in from outside, yippi-yay yippi-oh...

Translated from the German by Daniel Binswanger Friedman

Fragments of *The Lemberg Machine*

Dana Kavelina

169

It transpired like so. Then. Before everything.
There were no boundaries at first. There was
nothing. Boundaries between things only appeared
because God wanted to be a witness. After all, it's
impossible to be a witness to yourself, impossible
if . . . if there's nothing else. That is, if there's
nothing at all. There is only nothing. Only the
infinite in itself. Abiding. Always. It is impossible
to bear witness if there is only nothingness. In
order for the witness to arrive, time must first be
made. There must be a time and a place. Here.
There. Then. A witness cannot appear in the never.
Into the infinite. And time appears when there
is death. The end. Finite things, things with their
limits. Things that don't want to transgress their
boundaries, things that linger in them. Death must
be invented. So, first, you have to invent life, which
is almost the same thing. It was difficult.

He had to expel himself from himself. Inward.
To God. To what came before him. Nothingness
was banished into itself, compressed. The
ultimate form of expulsion. Not from here, but
here, deeper into itself, becoming less so that
something else could appear. Where there used
to be fullness. To become a witness: the ultimate
catastrophe. Because witnessing yourself out
of yourself is impossible. It takes another, with
another name to make a rigorous judgment
to define objects, names, and something like a
human being, someone who would at least fit the
role. A kind of person. With a name. So you can
testify to the witness. Testify about him. About
the witness. By pretending that it's a trial. Then,
there might be mercy. Not before the trial, but
after. First comes catastrophe, then comes mercy,
becoming a witness, seeking mercy in a damaged
world, picking up the pieces. There is endless
time to look for mercy in the dust, endless time to
fix and clear the dust. To fix things, to return from
exile. Someday. Maybe.

171

* * *

" … Mrs. Novitskaya … what's wrong with
our dear auntie, I wonder … And who is Mrs.
Novitskaya dragging by the hair? … It's a girl she's
dragging, the neighbors' girl. Screaming with that
huge mouth of hers, and how wide it opens. And
her teeth! Look at her teeth … Like a royal crown.
What is it that makes her laugh so much, I wonder
… what is it that makes her laugh so hard …?"

"Mama, mama, why was the first beggar blind?"
"That, my dear, is because he could see another
world, his eyes weren't meant for this one, but for
one that existed for less than a moment. That's
why his eyes could barely make out the things of
our world … And that was only right. He wasn't
blind, he had the best eyesight of all. Do you
understand? Sit still."

"It's been here all along. Before. Hidden. Now it's
showing its face. The beating. There it is."

"Mama, mama, why was the other beggar deaf?"
"Because he could only hear the sounds
of another world, and not this one. He was
completely deaf to this world because you can't
make out anything in it, just listen to them … the
screaming of the humiliated. He couldn't hear any
singing. So the beggar heard nothing. He heard
other things. Some beautiful things, I guess."

"Mama, and why was the third beggar a
stutterer?"
"He was not a stutterer at all. It was just hard for
him to say the words of this world: they were not
praise, they were ugly. Listen to the words of this
world. They shout 'Jew-communists.' Actually, he
didn't stutter at all, on the contrary—nobody in
the world spoke so fluently. When he sang songs,

172

all living things stopped in their tracks. He doesn't sing, and everything living is noisy and anxious ..."

* * *

"Remember what you explained to me the other day about the general strike? You said that the world would change irrevocably the moment everyone stopped at the same time. That everything would shift. That all of existence would be freed all at once. That everything would suddenly find its true colors. That it would all be made right. For such a correction to happen, a stop is essential. A general strike. The genocide will suddenly stop because there will be no one left to go to work. The cane will stop beating. The bullet will refuse to fly. Childbirth will cease. Rest will be manifested in all things.

"All things will belong to themselves, freed from belonging. A process of universal unmasking will occur. All possessions will become nobody's property. Things will belong to themselves. No man's land. Ground zero roadblock.

"A continual process of mutual forfeiture. Revolution. The unmaking of the world. Commons without grounds.
"Only the empty grave will remain in place and will not undergo rectification, because it is already rectified, free beforehand, because it already belongs to everyone.
"The empty grave is a strike! A continuous stoppage, owned by all!"

* * *

— Are you sure you want to eat all the bread now?
— ...
— Better split it into two halves. Eat one now and the other tomorrow.

173

— But in the morning we'll be off to the
   firing squad!
— You can eat it on the way.

"Don't be afraid. Just repeat to yourself:
'I am a crumb of bread, a yeast baby, I am less
than tiny. For me, a grain of sand for me is a giant,
I am a tiny little crumb, and no bullet will hit me,
it will pass me by, I myself will fall, fly away, and
dwell forever under the ground. The ants will be
my older brothers. The grass roots will become
high shtetls, there will be many like me, I'll
forever run away from you and hide, I'm a bread
crumb, you'll never find me, not even the birds
will find me, because I'm a bread crumb, you'll
call me and I'll pretend I didn't hear because
bread crumbs can't hear crude human voices.'"

* * *

"With livid tears I wash my bed, for I know that
my heart hides my neighbor's betrayal, for I
already have a clump of his hair in my hand, for
my mouth bears the traits of a dog's maw, full
of lies, and the keen eye can clearly see a filthy
mutt's fangs between my teeth.

"And may I never lay hands on daggers, for I
have it in me to slay my own mother if she takes
the enemy's side.

"And may no special conditions be bestowed
upon me, that I may prosper more than my
neighbor. May I never see a time of great temptation in which I might be enticed to hide my
oppression by oppressing my neighbors, to veil
my blackness by blackening them, to covet my
neighbor's house and his riches.

174

"May the Lord bind heavy stones upon my tongue
and upon my finger in the moment of reckoning,
lest I put my neighbor's son to the dogs, when
they come after him and howl over the city. For my
forefinger shall be thrust toward his door, for my
tongue shall be turned toward his name.

"May I never be tasked with drawing borders, for
there is a border that runs through the body of
the living, a border that cuts off the stomach from
the esophagus, a boundary that cuts off the leg
from the foot. For I know how to wipe the map off
the map, to blot out the names of strangers, when
they do not belong to the book of the names of
my people. For I have it in me to take a woman by
force, if her name is not written in the book of the
names of my people.

"May there never be sent unto me a time of
purging vengeance. For I will want to repay the evil
done to my ancestors by their ancestors. For I will
not know when to stop.

"May the Lord quiet the din of nations, for as soon
as the nations begin to make noise, the din drowns
out the cries of their victims, and then there is no
body count over the mass grave. May the Lord send
me mist instead of clear sunshine. May the Lord
send me confusion of mind.

"May the Lord send me and my people oppression
if it is possible to choose. For cursed are the sons
of the oppressors of the people, in the hellfire of
their mothers, their throats a needle's eye at the
feast of angels.

"May God grant me an exclusion so that I may not
be among those who exclude. That I may not be
the one with a rifle at the firing wall, but the victim
awaiting the end.

175

"For they will remember me as a martyr according to the merits of my suffering. And they will carry flowers to my monument until the end of time.

"For if my name be among the firing squad, my children shall curse it, and my grave shall sink into the mud at the end of time, when my victims' graves shall rise into the clearest air."

Translated from the Russian and Ukrainian by David Riff

The Lemberg Machine (2023)

Film by Dana Kavelina
Director of photography: Mikhail Chelnokov
Prop makers / decorators: Anna Nykytyuk,
Olena Golubova, Dana Kavelina
Animators: Olena Golubova, Dana Kavelina
Music: Mikhail Lylov

Commissioned by steirischer herbst '23
Produced by steirischer herbst '23 and
Dana Kavelina
With the kind support of ERSTE Foundation

Editors' Biographies

Ekaterina Degot is an art historian, researcher, and curator focusing on aesthetic and sociopolitical issues in Russia and Eastern Europe from the 19th century to the post-Soviet era. She began her tenure as director and chief curator of steirischer herbst in 2018. From 2014 to 2017, Degot was artistic director of the Academy of the Arts of the World in Cologne. Among other shows, she curated the First Ural Industrial Biennial in Yekaterinburg (2010, with Cosmin Costinas and David Riff) and headed the first Bergen Assembly with David Riff (2013).

David Riff is a writer, translator, artist, curator, and former member of the art group Chto Delat. He has been a curator at steirischer herbst since 2018. Among other shows, Riff cocurated the First Ural Industrial Biennial in Yekaterinburg (2010, with Cosmin Costinas and Ekaterina Degot) and headed the first Bergen Assembly together with Ekaterina Degot (2013). His most recent effort as an artist-curator was a large-scale exhibition on Mikhail Lifshitz in Moscow (2018, with Dmitry Gutov).

Contributors' Biographies

Ilya Budraitskis is a political and social theorist. His articles on Russian politics, culture, and intellectual history have been published in academic journals as well as in media outlets. Previously based in Moscow, he is currently a visiting scholar at the University of California, Berkeley. He is the author of *Dissidents among Dissidents: Ideology, Politics and the Left in Post-Soviet Russia* (Verso, 2022).

Mark Cinkevich is an interdisciplinary researcher and artist. In his practice, he is interested in critical, speculative, and experimental aspects of art that operate at the intersection of fact and fiction. His work focuses on the post-Soviet infrastructural and social landscape, through which he explores in particular the concepts of nuclear colonialism, infrastructural colonialism, extractivism, and monstrosity.

Anna Engelhardt is the alias of a research-based artist and writer. Her investigative practice spans multiple forms of media, including video, software, and hardware interfaces. Interested in the politics and history of information wars, she works with the tension between evidence and fiction, looking into subjects from military cybernetics to cyber warfare. Engelhardt has shown her work at festivals, galleries, and biennials and published in numerous journals.

Simona Forti is a professor of political philosophy at the Scuola Normale Superiore, Pisa. She is widely recognized for her studies on Hannah Arendt, the philosophical idea of totalitarianism, the relation between forms of power and subjectivities, and biopolitics. Her books include *New Demons: Rethinking Power and Evil Today* (2014) and *Totalitarianism: A Borderline Idea in Political Philosophy* (2024), both published by Stanford University Press.

Franziska Füchsl is a writer and literary translator. Her book *Tagwan* (Ritter, 2020) was nominated for the Rauriser Prize and the Clemens Brentano Prize. A second prose book, *Die Straßen sind sichtbar* (Ritter), was published in 2023, and her debut, *Rätsel in großer Schrift* (Edition Mosaik), in 2018. For her work, Füchsl has been awarded the Rotahorn and Heimrad Bäcker advancement awards and the Province of Styria's Morgenstern Prize. She is a member of the association Versatorium – Verein für Gedichte und Übersetzen.

Orit Halpern is professor and chair of digital cultures at Technische Universität Dresden. Her work bridges the histories of science, computing, and cybernetics with design. Halpern's first monograph, *Beautiful Data: A History of Vision and Reason* (Duke University Press, 2015), investigates histories of big data, design, and governmentality. Her latest book *The Smartness Mandate* (MIT Press, 2022), cowritten with Robert Mitchell, traces our obsession with smart technologies and artificial intelligence.

Dana Kavelina is an artist and filmmaker who works mainly with animation and video, but also with installation, painting, and graphics. Her works often address military violence and war from a gender perspective. They are particularly concerned with the position of the victim as a political subject, as well as the distance between historical and individual trauma. Kavelina's works are almost universally

based on her own poetry and
prose texts, which she weaves into
complex visual-linguistic forms.

S. Jonathon O'Donnell is a
specialist in American religious
and cultural studies, with a focus
on demonization, sovereign power,
and the religious right. They are
currently a visiting scholar at Queen's
University Belfast as well as an
adjunct assistant professor at Trinity
College Dublin and the University
of Leeds. Their first monograph,
*Passing Orders: Demonology and
Sovereignty in American Spiritual
Warfare* (Fordham University
Press), was published in 2021.

Roman Osminkin is a poet, art
and literary theorist, as well as
a playwright who works with
monumental ideological strata:
communism, liberalism, war,
nationalism, fascism, imperialism,
religion, etc. He is also a performer
between music and the spoken word,
having politicized the techniques of
Post-Conceptualism toward activism
and leftist emancipatory practices.
With the artist and writer Anastasia
Vepreva, Osminkin has recently
published the autoethnographic book
Kommunalka on Petrogradka (Novoe
Literaturnoe Obozrenie, 2022).

Peter Strasser is a philosopher and
retired professor at the University
of Graz. Between 1990 and 1995,
he was on the advisory board of
steirischer herbst. He is a regular
newspaper columnist and has
published numerous books, most
recently *Eine Hölle voller Wunder:
Spätes Philosophieren* (Sonderzahl,
2020) and *Apokalypse und Advent:
Warum wir dagewesen sein werden*
(Sonderzahl, 2022). In 2014, he
was awarded the Austrian State
Prize for Cultural Journalism.

steirischer herbst '23 Festival Team

Ekaterina Degot
Director and Chief Curator

Rita Puffer
Chief Financial Officer

Theresa Weiler
Director's Office

David Riff
Senior Curator

Pieternel Vermoortel
Senior Curator

Gábor Thury
Curator

Beatrice Forchini
Assistant Curator

Tobias Ihl
Assistant Curator

Barbara Seyerl
Assistant Curator /
University Programs

Judith Brand
Head of Communications

Martina Heil
Communications

Luca Rädler
Communications

Vesna Pajičić
Visitor Service / Communications /
Artist Coordination

Jeff Thoss
Editor

Fotini Lazaridou-Hatzigoga
Website

Christina Kasic
Sponsoring/Funding

Dietmar Reinbacher
Head of herbst education / Outreach

Lena Riecnik
herbst education / Artist Coordination

Markus Plasencia
herbst education for Schools

Jakob Schweighofer
Head of Production

Roland Gfrerer
Production

Martin Pelzmann
Production

Karl Masten
Technical Management

Peter Schloss
Exhibition Design

Jacqueline Meixner
Guest and Production Office

Marlene Obermayer
Head of Archive/Library

Carina Hutter
Archive/Library

Stefanie Lazarus
Office Management

Matthias Ulbl
Accounting

Kathrin Lazarus
Personnel/Accounting

Simon Resch
Office Assistant

Danica Radat
Facility Management

Grupa Ee (Mina Fina, Damjan
Ilić, Ivian Kan Mujezinović)
Design

Systemantics
Web Development

Festival Support

Communications
Henrik Bergstedt
Janosch Böhm
Miles Borghese
Reinhold Kuhne
Birgit Polzer
Oliver Possenig
Helene Prvinsek
Thomas Schober

Visitor Service
Evgeniia Kachmazova
Moritz Müller
Olgica Perić
Stefanie Schweiger
Edvin Smajić
Melanie Wolf
Paul Wolff
Eva Zückert

Education
Romina Gollob
Kim Groneweg
Laurenz Henkel
Julia Robin
Klara Schmidt
Lisa Schmidt
Marion Winter

Production
Miriam Bacher
A. Tolga Baci
Lukas Bayer
Zoe Borzi
Elsa Chinese
Ahmad Darkhabani
Madeleine Dietrichstein
Maxine Fabian
Ines El Foutati
Florentina Freiding
Nicolas Pleasure Galani
Eduardo Gracia Garcia
Andreas Grantner
Gottfried Gratzer
Christina Hahn
Marlena Hahn
Valentin Hasebe
Hanna Hofmann
Philipp Hofmann
Shirin Hooshmandi

Cosima Hubner
Christian Jalen
Jelena Jovovic
Lukas Kaiser
Natalie Kirchmair
Anna Christina Köberl
Katarina Kostelac
Heinz Leitner
Magdalena Linhart
Inka Martinovic
Jasmin Murtinger
Marharyta Muzyka
Maria-Oscara Ohrenstein
Lucie Olet
Lorenzo Orsenico
Lieselotte Payer
Darius Petrovic
Marc Pietkiewicz
Ylvi Pilinger
Felicitas Pilz
Ronny Priesching
Thomas Anselm Probstmeier
Julia Purgstaller
Eva Schmartschan
Guggi Schneider
Andreas Schögler
Anna Sudy
Carmen Suppan
Julia Thurner
Diana Carolina Torres Salazal
Nedim Vejo
Gregor Wahl
Barbara Zambo

Colophon

This book is published in conjunction with steirischer herbst festival steirischer herbst '23—*Humans and Demons*, September 21–October 15, 2023, Graz, Styria, Austria.

This edition of steirischer herbst was curated by Ekaterina Degot, David Riff, Pieternel Vermoortel, Gábor Thury, Barbara Seyerl, and Mirela Baciak and created by the whole team of steirischer herbst.

Editors:
Ekaterina Degot
David Riff

With contributions by:
Ilya Budraitskis, Anna Engelhardt and Mark Cinkevich, Simona Forti, Franziska Füchsl, Orit Halpern, Dana Kavelina, S. Jonathon O'Donnell, Roman Osminkin, Peter Strasser

Managing editor:
Jeff Thoss

Proofreading:
Aaron Bogart

Graphic design and typesetting:
Grupa Ee (Mina Fina, Damjan Ilić, Ivian Kan Mujezinović)

Typefaces:
Mercure
Studio Pro

Production:
Thomas Lemaître, Hatje Cantz

Printing:
Livonia Print Ltd., Riga

Paper:
Grenita, 250 g/m²
Munken Print White 15, 90 g/m²

© 2024 Hatje Cantz Verlag, Berlin, steirischer herbst, Graz, and authors

© 2023 Anna Engelhardt and Mark Cinkevich for the reproduced stills from *Onset*

The automated analysis of this work in order to obtain information, in particular about patterns, trends, and correlations, is prohibited in accordance with § German 44b UrhG ("text and data mining").

steirischer herbst festival gmbh
Sackstraße 17
8010 Graz, Austria
www.steirischerherbst.at

Published by
Hatje Cantz Verlag GmbH
Mommsenstraße 27
10629 Berlin, Germany
www.hatjecantz.com
A Ganske Publishing Group Company

ISBN 978-3-7757-5828-4

Printed in Latvia

Cover illustration:
Grupa Ee

Every effort has been made to trace the copyright holders and obtain permission to reproduce material. Please do get in touch with any inquiries or any information relating to unintended omissions.